To Carol
I hope you
enjoy it.

All My Patients Have Tales

Why Veterinary Medicine is a True Calling

Jeff Wells, DVM

Illustrations by **June Camerer**

Text copyright © 2006 Jeff Wells, DVM
Illustration copyright © 2006 June Camerer
All rights reserved.
Printed in U.S.A. by Sheridan Books on acid-free paper

Hadley Inc.

P.O. Box 1353 • Conifer, CO 80433

www.allmypatientshavetails.com

ISBN 0-9787169-0-6 (soft cover)
ISBN 0-9787169-1-4 (hard cover)

10 9 8 7 6 5 4 3 2   First printing 2006

Design by: F + P Graphic Design, Inc.

Contents

Feline Frenzy

Mrs. Perkins was methodically explaining the symptoms that her new cat, Henry, was experiencing. Although she hadn't had him long enough to know him well, she said it was obvious he wasn't feeling up to par. Mrs. Perkins was a vibrant blonde in her early thirties with the typical Dakota accent. Her husband traveled a lot with his job, and she was elated to have a fuzzy new companion.

She looked me up and down skeptically, clearly evaluating the new guy on the block. I had only been out of veterinary school for a few months. I'm sure it was more apparent than I would have wanted to admit that I was still a little nervous about every case that walked through the door, afraid that I might not be able to handle the situation or that I might misdiagnose the ailment of a beloved pet.

"I just picked him up from the Humane Society two days ago and he was fine then, don'tcha know," Mrs. Perkins began. "Then last night he began to howl when he went to use the litter box. It was the most horrible noise I have ever heard a kitty make. You've just got to help him."

Even though I was a novice, I had a pretty good idea what was afflicting the recently adopted feline. "Do you know why he ended up at the Humane Society, Mrs. Perkins?"

She pondered for a moment before responding. "You betcha, I remember now—they said he was urinating on the owners' carpet the last couple weeks."

These were the classic signs of a urinary infection, and the howling indicated that a bladder stone was now blocking Henry's urethra, making it nearly impossible for him to empty his bladder. I would need to palpate the bladder to see how full it was and take an x-ray to locate the exact location of the blockage. Henry was still in the blue plastic carrier that Mrs. Perkins brought him in. I set it on the Formica exam table between us.

I opened the metal grate door and began to ease my hand in to get a hold of the patient. My hand was almost to the cat's head when his new owner remembered an important piece of information. "Oh, Doctor, I almost forgot—Henry is practically feral. You can't pet him or pick him up. I had to coax him into the carrier with food and slam the door." This was definitely information I could have used earlier! Now I stood frozen with my arm elbow-deep in the cage of an uncivil feline. On instinct my hand began to pull back, but it was too late. A sharp pain shot up my arm, and the familiar sensation of warm blood washed over my palm. Henry had sunk his teeth into my index finger.

A white furry tornado then spun out the door of the carrier, tearing at my forearm as it made an escape. Henry hit the floor at a dead run and slid on the linoleum tile as he rounded the corner, disappearing out the doorway of the exam room. Still in shock from my own injuries, I bent over holding my damaged limb against my abdomen and held back words that would be unacceptable in rural South Dakota. Mrs. Perkins began to tear up. "Oh, Henry! Please don't let him get hurt or escape outdoors," she pleaded. "He's so fragile."

This statement brought me back to my senses, imagining how upset Mrs. Perkins would be if Henry did manage to make it outside

or got hurt trying. I took off after the frightened feline, temporarily forgetting my shredded hand.

Henry had made it into the reception area and immediately started climbing the curtains. Determined to bolt, he seemed to have reached a maximum level of hysteria, spewing excrement randomly as he scurried from drape to drape. The question I frantically pondered was how to get a hold of the neurotic cat without exciting him even more or losing a limb in the process. While I stood in the middle of the room wondering why this situation had never been described to me in veterinary school, he made a full circle by using the curtain rods as a trapeze set, then disappeared into the next room.

Mrs. Perkins yelped as Henry streaked by her in the hallway and made for the laboratory, the one room with the most potential for damage by an over-stimulated kitty. Following the trail of rancid diarrhea and wondering how the intestinal tract of just one 10-pound cat could possibly produce so much, I followed him into the lab. By this point I felt sure that Henry was displaying some as-yet-undiscovered biologic mechanism that generated an infinite amount of fecal material because it now blanketed the once-pristine counter-tops and sterile instruments in the room. The only good news was that he had decided to take a hiatus behind the autoclave and peered out at me from behind it. His pupils were wide open with fear, and the backs of his eyes reflected the florescent lighting, giving them a greenish-yellow glow. He sat still as a statue, like young deer or rabbits when approached in the deep grass, seeming to believe "If I don't move, the human won't see me."

Now I had to decide how I was to get a hold of Henry without making the room even more of a disaster zone. For the lack of a more brilliant plan, I turned to the basics: "Kitty, kitty, kitty," I called, trying to sound as loving as possible under the circumstances. It didn't work. These words only seemed to alert the statuesque feline that I could actually see him, jolting him back into action across the countertop. "Oh, no, not those!" I hollered, but it was too late. The 30-plus blood tubes that we had worked so hard to get from the unwilling 200-pound pigs the previous afternoon crashed to the floor with just a little shove from Henry. It had taken hours to extract the blood for viral testing. My inexperience combined with the determination of the hefty porcine had provided a year's worth of entertainment for the farmer and his neighbors. Now I would have to call him, explain the situation and endure the ridicule of another trip to the farm. I could already picture the scene: even more locals would be invited this time. Chairs would probably be set up and maybe even tickets sold. But first I still had to retrieve this cat.

I decided then that I had had enough. Henry made for the door to exit the lab, but I stood my ground. This time he hesitated, giving me that crucial split second. I dove and scooped him up, keeping his glistening white teeth at bay. He wiggled and clawed at me, making his way up my shoulder. Then he abruptly stopped moving and appeared to relax. He was hanging by one paw from my earlobe. The razor-sharp claws had punctured the fleshy portion of my ear deeply enough to support his weight. I don't know if he had finally given up from exhaustion or just decided to claim victory, but it seemed that someone turned off his switch.

When Mrs. Perkins found us, her reaction was not what I might have wished. Instead of, "I'm so sorry—are you OK, Doctor?" she said, "Oh, you haven't injured my Henry, have you?"

With the feline still attached to my ear, blood running down my neck and Mrs. Perkins scolding me about proper pet restraint, I began to reflect on what exactly had brought me to this point. Eight years of strenuous college curriculum, national board exams, and a huge student loan debt all added up to this glamorous title of veterinarian that I had coveted for most of my life.

I wondered what my friends from college were doing now. Probably sitting in plush offices, making big bucks and working with clients who didn't regularly bite them, I guessed. Yet I really do enjoy this sometimes crazy career choice of mine, and I can't imagine not having chosen it even though I'm not always appreciated by owner or patient.

So why did I decide to become a veterinarian? It isn't an easy path; it requires years of hard work just to get that Doctor of Veterinary Medicine degree to hang on a wall, followed by long hours for moderate compensation once you've got a wall to hang it on. To explain myself, I think I'd better start from the beginning.

Humble Beginnings

At least once a week I am presented with a young boy or girl who wishes to become a veterinarian. These kids' parents are often standing proudly behind them, beaming from ear to ear. These future vets always have a great love for animals and a deep sense of dedication. But I have to choke back the urge to awaken them to the long, arduous training and all-nighters that lay ahead of them before they will actually be able to heal an animal. Usually, I just gather a smile and pat them on the head, wishing them the best of luck. I always visualize a little of myself in these eager faces, reminding me of why I longed to become a veterinarian and what got me through those eight years of college.

To understand what led me down this wild road, we have to flash back to my childhood. I grew up in a small farming community in southeastern Iowa. On the edge of the Bible Belt, it was not a big tourist destination, but it sure was a great place to be a kid. It's the kind of place where most everyone knows everybody else and people really do take care of each other. Retail shops surrounded a picturesque town square with a bandstand in the center. Weekly instrumental concerts filled steamy summer evenings, and townspeople enjoyed the music from the comfort of strategically placed lawn chairs. It was a town that might have inspired Norman Rockwell, and it hasn't changed all that much in the last 40 years.

We lived on a small "hobby farm" just outside of town where I kept almost every type of pet at one time or another. Cats, dogs, horses, cows, sheep, and even pigs sometimes ended up on our little acreage. Active in the local 4-H club, my sisters and I proudly showed off our menagerie at the county and state fairs in late summer. Fortunately, my father made a living teaching agriculture at the high school, so we didn't have to count on our animals for income like the real farmers.

My favorites in our collection were a Saint Bernard named Heidi and a white Welsh pony named Midge. Heidi and I logged many hours of roughhousing that usually ended in her pinning my shoulders

onto the lush lawn with her front paws, then bathing me in saliva with her immense tongue. This was before canine oral care had gained popularity, sending me straight for the shower before sitting down for dinner.

Midge spent most days grazing in belly-deep grass pastures, but she always rose to the occasion when she was asked. She could be ridden without a saddle or bridle. You could just jump on her back and take off for a ride across the property, no tack required. Midge was also a big draw on grade school field trips. Our class would fill up a school bus and head for the petting zoo we called home. Everyone got a ride on Midge, and she was more than happy to oblige. Kids would fall off and even end up underneath her, but she would just stop and wait for them to get back on. These days, of course, insurance companies would never allow such activities for school kids.

Growing up around all these animals it was easy for me to answer the age-old question of "What do you want to be when you grow up?" with "A veterinarian, of course." Conveniently, the local veterinary clinic was less than a quarter of a mile from our house. I got a job cleaning kennels at the clinic after school and spent available weekends riding along on farm calls. Soon I was hooked and there seemed to be no other logical career path.

I'm sure my teachers felt there was no way that I would ever be able to make the grades required to get into veterinary school, but sometimes being told you can't do something makes you even more determined to get it done When it came time to graduate from high school and head for college, I was filled with anticipation. I arrived at Iowa State University determined that with a little hard work I could make the cut, but I was in for a big surprise. Reality hit when I opened the new campus phone book soon after I arrived and was completely set back by what I saw.

It seemed that almost every other freshman student in the university phone book was a pre-vet, too There must have been thousands of them, and Iowa State's veterinary college only accepted about 80 in-state students every year of the 120 total. My heart fell as I turned the pages and began to wonder what my second choice for a career might be. After a couple hours of couch time spent staring blankly at the television in utter dejection, I mustered the energy to crawl into bed. With the covers pulled over my face, I came to the realization that I had already purchased all the books for my pre-vet classes, and I'd spent years telling everyone that I wanted to be a veterinarian. So for now, I decided, I had to at least give it a try.

The first couple of years involved lots of chemistry, physics and many other assorted "weed-out" classes. Many of my fellow students had what seemed to me a truly amazing ability to act like they had everything under control. These people did what I now know was such a great job of putting on a front that I was certain I was the only one who was struggling, even when using every available minute to study.

Once, after a big physics test during my sophomore year, I noticed a girl standing at the bulletin board pondering the test scores. I had been looking for an excuse to talk to her for over a year and took this opportunity to do so. She was very attractive and exuded confidence, making it extra hard to initiate a conversation. "Tough exam, how did you do?" I managed to get out while staring safely at the computerized spreadsheet taped to the wall.

There was an uncomfortable silence. I began to assume she had no interest in talking to me when she breathed a deep sigh and turned towards me. Her eyes were misty, and tears began to spill down her face. In a matter-of-fact tone she declared, "Well, that's it for me. I've gotten D's on all the exams in this class, and my grade point can't take it. No veterinary school for me." I was shocked. She had always appeared to be a confident shoo-in, but all was not as it appeared. Concluding that this probably wasn't the best time to ask her out, we went are separate ways and I never saw her again.

Towards the end of our junior year, it was finally time to send in our applications for veterinary school. This meant taking the Medical College Admittance Test, the same exam taken by medical school hopefuls and the longest two days of my life. It was one of those exams that actually shortens your lifespan—at least I think it did mine. Put a few hundred extremely nervous pre-professional students in one lecture hall and you can practically smell the tension. I was nauseous for most of the 48 hours, especially when realizing there were entire pages of questions about which I was completely clueless. This accounted for areas on my answer sheet where the filled-in dots formed an assortment of geometric patterns that I'm fairly sure had nothing to do with the correct answers.

A few months later The Letter from the Iowa State College of Veterinary Medicine appeared in my mail slot. I stood staring at it, wondering if not knowing was better than knowing and being disappointed. Realizing that someday it would have to be opened, I tore into the envelope. "This letter is to inform you that you have…not been accepted for next year's freshman class."

I wanted to just put it back in the mailbox and ignore the fact that I knew. But it was too late—the genie was out of the bottle, and now I had the terrible task of telling my parents and friends. Everyone else took it better than I did, and even though I wanted to run away and become a ski bum, I decided to give it another try.

I learned later that without a bachelor's degree, getting accepted the first try was almost impossible for anyone. In fact, several applicants already had master's degrees. A year later, after completing my Animal Science degree, the envelope contained a much better answer. It was a day of celebration in my blissful ignorance of what lay ahead the following fall. √

Veterinary School:
Put My Hand Where?

F our years of undergraduate work, constantly stressing about keeping a high enough grade point average to be accepted, culminated in my finally arriving at that mythical first day of veterinary school. I sat in the last and top row of the stark freshman lecture hall. The chairs were Early American plastic attached to imitation wooden desks barely large enough to hold a piece of notebook paper. The dean was explaining the rules and regulations of the school while the front-row crowd was frantically taking notes. They were at it already, the same students who had raised the curve in my pre-vet classes back on the main campus. Which of the dean's general remarks could possibly need to be written down, I wondered. These front-row students were working hard to impress the "right people" early on. As it turned out, these attitudes and seating arrangements would remain the same for the next four years.

The veterinary school was well over a mile from the heart of the university. The building was immense and partly below ground, which is where freshmen were kept for most of their first year. It was constructed of concrete block with just enough windows to remind us what sunlight was like. The stark white walls were interrupted periodically by orange metal doorways and bad seventies art. The school was completely self-contained, everything under one flat roof. (I always wondered who thought flat roofs were a good idea in high precipitation areas where they were constantly in need of maintenance—thus, the familiar smell of hot tar every spring.)

Most of the time it seemed we were completely isolated from the rest of the world. In some ways it was a lot like high school, equipped as it was with locker rooms and our own intramural teams. We would be with these same 120 people for almost half a decade, and some would become lifelong friends. We took all of our classes in the same building, studied there and occasionally slept there. I think we sometimes forgot we were allowed to leave.

As that first day of orientation dragged on, I couldn't wait for vet school to begin for real. A couple of upperclassmen wandered by the open door behind the podium where the dean was speaking. They smiled and shook their heads knowingly, well aware of what we were in for and just glad they didn't have to do it again. First-year classes were made up of the basics: anatomy, physiology, embryology and histology. Although these can be less than stimulating subjects, they do form the basis of an entire veterinary career.

The first day of any anatomy lab always brings with it the concern of how one will react to the cadavers. I was fortunate enough to have grown up around life and death in our little farming community, but some of my classmates were not so blessed. A few of the most affected bolted for the restroom while the rest of us spent most of that first lab holding back our gag reflex, trying to maintain an image of coolness in front of our new cohorts and competitors. After a few weeks dissection became more routine, and we settled into the first year.

One class that first year most of us never really got used to. It was physiology, taught by a German immigrant, Dr. Andre Kaiser. He was a very intelligent man who had an extremely hard time getting his point across. Always in excellent physical shape for a man in his early sixties, Andre often sported tight T-shirts and shorts to impress the girls in the class, plus a perfectly coiffed head of gray hair and matching goatee to top off his superior appearance. Clogs were inevitably his choice of footwear no matter how deep the snow outside. (I've never trusted men who wear clogs since then.) Even though Dr. Kaiser had lived in this country for several years, he still maintained a very thick accent and seemed to take advantage of it to further confuse the students. Most of us got the feeling that he was not there to teach so much as to provide us with hardship and stress. This proved to be true when, after the first exam, he paraded around the room like a rooster, not able to restrain his glee in the fact that less than half of us were even able to squeak out a "C" Many of us thought this class might be our last, so after abandoning the idea of shipping him back from whence he came, someone suggested we form study groups just to decipher his lectures. This game plan worked well, saving many panicked freshmen from an early defeat. Looking back, I wonder if his original plan was to make life hard enough to bring us together. Whatever the intention, after Kaiser's torment, a more cooperative and less cutthroat attitude dominated our study habits.

The rest of that first year provided us with a continual flow of extremely helpful and devoted professors. They all seemed to feel that their particular subject was the one we couldn't live without, no matter how impractical it might be in the real world of veterinary practice. I can still remember the names of a multitude of exotic diseases only found in the most remote areas of Africa.

The freshman year ended in a flurry of final exams that pushed each one of us to the limits of our mental and physical capacities. I opted to put off studying for my last exam, which happened to by in histology, to concentrate on the other subjects first. Unfortunately, this left me looking at an all-nighter.

The histology final was two hours long, spent mostly staring into a microscope. About halfway through, every student's worst nightmare happened to me: I actually fell asleep during the test. My eyeballs pressed against the optics of the microscope. I still have no idea how much time passed during my nap, but when I awoke, a feeling of panic swelled over me. Searching the room for a clock through my groggy daze, all I could see was my fellow students busily analyzing the glass slides that had been specifically prepared for the exam. I scrambled to finish evaluating the cells that we had spent the last year fretting over, barely finishing when the professor called time. The little siesta cost me the grade I had hoped for, but at least I hadn't missed the whole thing.

It's been many years since that awful experience, but up until the last couple of years I would still occasionally wake up in a cold sweat, sure that I had missed my finals all together or forgotten to go to a specific class for an entire semester. I think of it as my own personal version of post-traumatic stress syndrome.

Our sophomore year was probably the toughest scholastically, but having one year under our belts made it a little easier to adjust. We also had gotten to know each other well enough to know who our friends were and who might be out for themselves only. Classes like pharmacology, microbiology and virology dominated the scene. You know it's a tough year when crying is a regular occurrence after reading the posted test scores. But we held on, wading through it with the knowledge that the junior year would bring more practicality and hands-on experience.

The third year did bring more practicality. We even got to work with animals in some of our classes, such as reproduction lab. Pregnancy diagnosis is an important part of almost every veterinarian's career in both small and large animal practice, so this was an important introduction. Unfortunately, with large animals pregnancy diagnosis always involves a long plastic glove. We were dressed in our brand-new, clean white coveralls with smart veterinary emblems sewn on the right chest region. A potentially pregnant cow was placed in front of each student as we took our turn one by one to make a determination.

The girl beside me was particularly nervous about this task as she had not been around cattle before that day. She whispered in my ear right before her turn came, "I only want to work on cats and dogs. I really don't care to do this." Eventually her turn came to give it a try. An extremely large Holstein cow was led in front of her while she put on a large plastic glove and lubed up her arm. She placed it inside the cow as far as she could. As luck would have it, the patient had spent the last couple of weeks on a particularly lush Iowa pasture and was anything but constipated. By this time my fellow student had her shoulder actually inside the cow, making the beast a little agitated. Finally, the immense bovine arched her back and directed all the abdominal pressure she could muster to forcing the student's arm out of her for good.

But my comrade was more determined than one might think, not easily yielding to the cow's wishes. Her arm must have been positioned at just the perfect angle because an explosive stream of pungent green liquid stool found its target on my classmate's face. She was temporarily transformed into the Creature from the Black Lagoon One would have to assume that a small amount made it into her mouth, but I never brought it up. We all felt very sorry for her, but she was able to laugh about it after a couple weeks of utter humiliation.

Our senior year was split between the clinics at the school and working in actual veterinary practices. We came and went from the school to the "real world" and back again. During our time at the school we saw patients before our professors did, trying to make the correct diagnoses while still under experienced supervision. Working in this controlled environment, one of my classmates had an experience that affected his whole career.

He was seeing patients in the school clinics one afternoon when a client brought in an extremely uncomfortable German shepherd. The big dog's anal glands were impacted and required expressing to return him to normal. Anal gland expressing is not one of the more sought-out procedures by vets or their patients. For one thing, it usually takes a full day for the odor to completely leave the exam room.

We were just in the beginning stages of learning how to handle upset animals, more worried about making a good impression on the client and teacher than the animal's attitude. Barry lifted the dog's tail to examine the inflamed glands, and the next thing he knew the dog had wrapped his jaws around Barry's right arm. Worse yet, the dog refused to let go, and it took two other students to pry the animal off. Blood oozed from the deep punctures as Barry slammed the door on the exam room, running for the sink. His face was pale and sweating, while the rest of the his body shook uncontrollably. That day he decided to go into large animal practice exclusively.

As school began to wind down, we all started to think of leaving what was still at least a somewhat sheltered academic world. Most of us had put in at least eight tough years preparing for practice, but now that we were almost ready, it seemed like a scary prospect. Would we be successful or would we fail miserably? How could we possibly remember all the information that had been thrown at us over the years? One by one my fellow classmates started accepting jobs all around the country. We shared many sad good-byes, knowing that most of us would never cross paths again.

This time was hard for me and also made me nervous, inciting a desperate interviewing blitz. I looked at jobs from California to Maine but couldn't quite find the right fit. I had imagined myself leaving the Midwest, yet when a very intriguing offer came in from eastern South Dakota, I couldn't pass it up. The location didn't sound very glamorous, but I really liked the veterinarian who owned the practice, and the facilities were first-rate.

I decided to accept the position and packed up my red 1973 Mercury Marquis with all my belongings. This didn't amount to much: a lot of textbooks, a small, out-of-date wardrobe, and eight years' worth of college memories. It was the last time in life I could move all my belongings without a trailer or moving van—not necessarily a bad thing. I headed the Marquis in a northwesterly direction, eager but a little worried. I had no idea what I was in for.

Wide Open Spaces

The big car cruised easily across the open plains, hindered only by its constant appetite for gasoline. Crossing the Missouri River I felt the door close for the last time on my life as a boy in Iowa and open to the reality of a truly adult one. Once into South Dakota, the horizon flattened out, and the rare appearance of other cars on the interstate became a welcome sight. The wind started to pick up, and a small, familiar sign reminded me of where I was: it amounted to nothing more than a wooden stake attached to a horizontal board that read, "Wall Drug, 403 Miles." Memories of a family trip resurfaced. I had been by this sign many years before on one of those vacations as a teenager when you are completely embarrassed to be with your parents. The last place you want to be is locked in a car for hours with the family, so you behave like a jerk, making it hard for anyone to have a good time.

I pulled up to the vet clinic at dusk, with barely enough light left to recognize the buildings. The main structure was a split-level with offices in the lower level and living quarters on the upper floor.

Directly to the west of the converted house, about 30 feet away, sat a 50-foot square, one-story barn with stalls for keeping sick horses and a surgery area that included a hydraulic operating table for large animals.

A light in one of the basement offices let me know my new employer was waiting on me. I opened the white metal door and took a couple of steps down into the office area. A waiting room and reception area lay straight ahead, and a lab was to the right. The small animal surgery room, exam room and doctors' office were to the left. The entire floor was covered with the same yellow linoleum, badly scuffed from heavy boot traffic. The familiar smell of B vitamins filled the room; every veterinary clinic I've been in has smelled exactly the same way.

My new boss greeted me with a broad smile and firm hand shake, welcoming me into his practice and putting me at ease. He turned out to be as nice and honest a guy as you would ever want to meet. Now, after a lot of veterinary medicine under my belt, I realize what a risk it is to bring someone new into the fold. So many things could go wrong with a young veterinarian you barely know. The new associate could be over-confident yet ineffectual, causing clients to leave or, even worse, file a lawsuit. But he took a chance on me, and I still appreciate that he did.

"How was your trip? Do you need anything to eat?" he asked. Explaining that I was beat but appreciated the offer, I drove off to the studio basement apartment that I had found while interviewing a couple of weeks before. It wasn't much more than an oven, a 20-year-old avocado-green refrigerator and a bathroom, but it was more than I could really afford at $235 a month. By the time my $400-a-month student loan payments and health insurance came out of my $23,000-a-year paycheck, I knew there wouldn't be much left for food and essentials.

By the time I unpacked my microwave and few toiletry items, it was well after *Letterman* and time to get some sleep. I piled up clothes and threw a blanket over the top of the mound, which doubled as a mattress that first night. In the morning I would have to appear professional and be prepared to act like I knew what I was doing in front of my new boss. Lying on my temporary bed, I listened to the couple next door yelling at each other about her mother's upcoming visit and wondered how much more an above-ground apartment would cost per month.

I arrived at the clinic the next morning to start the first day of work, meet the staff and begin to learn the ropes. Pulling in the driveway at 7:45 in an attempt to make a good impression, I found the facility still fairly quiet with the steamy haze of a Midwestern morning just starting to blow off. My new employer said a quick hello as he passed, heading out to a full morning of farm calls, leaving me awkwardly trying to find something to do. I walked down into the office area and took a seat at what would be my desk. It was recently cleaned out, completely barren like a clean slate.

The outside door swung open just as I was contemplating what I might use to start filling up my inherited space. Through the door walked a young woman about 26 years old, medium build, five foot

five inches tall with shoulder length, thick, dark hair. She wore a light blue lab coat over gray overalls and sturdy brown leather work boots. Not the cover of *Vogue*, but a good practical outfit for veterinary practice. I stood up to introduce myself, and she began to look me over. Her eyes narrowed and her nose wrinkled. She was sizing me up, and I wondered how I was going to make out.

"Nice to meet you. I'm Jeff," I said, sticking out my hand.

She grasped it firmly, asserting her authority. "You must be the new guy," she replied with what seemed a tinge of disappointment in her voice. "I'm Jenny, your technician, and we'll be spending a lot of time together." What I was sure she was really thinking was, "Oh, boy, now I have to train this guy." She dropped my hand and spoke again "You won't actually be treating anything for the first month; you'll be working with the veterinarian whom you'll be replacing."

Ugh, a direct kick to the groin, leaving me with a pit in my stomach and no air left in my lungs. She was good—well-versed in putting young veterinarians in their place! Did she not understand the years I had spent preparing for this day? The sacrifices I had made? All-nighters at the vet school running I.V. fluids into vomiting dogs and sucking down caffeine while the professors slept peacefully in their beds? She didn't seem to have any appreciation for the hundreds of tests I had taken or the hours of preparation they required.

Yet, after I got my wind back, I realized that it was probably a good idea to get some on-the-job training. Besides, I could learn my way around the practice and get to know the clients. So I gave Jenny an accepting nod, and she took off to start her morning routine. This would not really be my first day of practice after all, but that day would come soon enough.

Baptism:
Reality Strikes Back

My first real day of practice as a licensed veterinarian was full of a little anticipation and a whole lot of fear. After eight years of preparation, it was finally "go time."

I had spent my first month at the practice with the veterinarian I was replacing, meeting the clients and trying to learn as much from her as possible. She was a highly respected veterinarian with an abundance of patience, fortunately for me. Dr. Ann had grown up in South Dakota and understood how to deal with the locals. She was barely over five feet tall but was in great shape, so even the most physical task did not appear to slow her down. Her hair was dark, wavy, and always kept short for easy maintenance, a logical style for a woman with such a messy occupation. The clients adored her, as did I.

Jewelry might easily get caught in the hair of a dog or the tail of a cow, so Dr. Ann never wore it. She was personable, honest and a very good practitioner, but she was joining a practice closer to her new family a couple of hours away. She had recently married and inherited two teenage daughters. Obviously, she had her work cut out for her. Dr. Ann would be sorely missed, and I understood that filling her shoes was going to be hard, even with my big feet.

I learned an awful lot from her in that month and became a little too comfortable in my role as her apprentice. As most young graduates from professional school, I thought that I had at last gained all the knowledge I needed to jump right into practice and save the world from disease and pestilence. As you can guess, I was in for a rude awakening. By the time my month of training with Dr. Ann was up, I was dying to get out there and give it a shot on my own. I figured that my employer, Dr. Dave, would always be there for guidance in my upcoming adventures On her last day Dr. Ann shook my hand and wished me luck with a knowing smile. She was all too aware of the challenges ahead of me in the next couple of months. She headed out onto the pavement and never looked back. The next morning I would be on my own.

I didn't sleep very well that night, trying to imagine myself in a multitude of situations that might occur the next day. I even tried counting sheep, but one of them ended up with a birthing problem that I couldn't remember how to deal with. At last morning came, and I hurried to get to the clinic early to see what my first tasks in the "real world" would be. This was the last day that I was ever early. I tried to appear casual as I strolled over to the reception desk to glance at my schedule. It began with pregnancy testing horses followed by a dog spay and an afternoon kept open to catch whatever emergencies came up. This sounded good, but I knew my afternoon was open because no one wanted to see the new guy. The people of eastern South Dakota did not accept change quickly. I would be under the community microscope for quite some time.

I headed out to the practice truck that I was taking over from Ann, shoved the seat back so I wouldn't be eating my knees and jumped in. Jenny crawled in beside me, and we started off the day I had so long anticipated. I peered through a kaleidoscope of glass—a windshield beaten by the South Dakota wind and too many gravel roads. The dashboard was stuffed with old receipts, syringe cases and the occasional candy wrapper. The seats were warped and threadbare, and the smell of antiseptic soaps and vitamins permeated the cab of the truck.

Pulling into the Weber farm I was a little nervous yet very excited about being the person they had hired to determine whether or not their mares were pregnant. I approached the house, passing a decomposing truck, rows of barbed wire and leaning out buildings. As at all agricultural operations in the heartland, this one had the obligatory four- to six-foot border of perfectly shorn grass along the drive, a border of order, defending the homestead from the ever-encroaching chaos of a livestock operation.

The Webers were a tough farm family. They worked very hard to make a living with a herd of about 30 prize quarter horse mares plus countless numbers of dairy cows and pigs. Mrs. Weber worked just as hard as her husband did, hooking the cows up to the milking machines and keeping the equipment clean. She was a small woman with salt-and-pepper hair. There was not an inch of body fat on her from running miles around the farm looking after her husband and the animals. Since both of their sons had left the farm to pursue careers that were more financially rewarding, they had to hire part-time help to plant and harvest the crops.

Like most farmers in the area, the Webers lived on the economic edge, so having their brood mares pregnant was very important. If the mares were bred they could go out to the far pastures; if not, they would need to spend more time with the stallion. Sometimes those that were "open," or not with foal, would even require medical treatment before they could hold a pregnancy. Mares that did not have foals the following spring would not help the Webers' financial situation. The pressure was on me to make the correct diagnoses, and the Webers were big fans of my predecessor, so this was my test run.

I slipped on the long, plastic palpation glove, without which I would never be able to get my fingernails clean again. Jenny held a gallon jug from which she dumped a large glob of gelatinous lubrication into my hand. The first mare stood ready in front of me, restrained in a palpation stock for her safety and mine. I eased my well-prepared hand into her rectum, feeling for the uterus that lay below. I had done this many times before in school or under the supervision of an experienced vet. But today was different. Instead of easily finding the uterus as before, everything inside the animal felt like unrecognizable mush. I couldn't find the uterus or the hard head of an equine fetus. I was taking too much time, and the Webers were starting to fidget. Even the horse began flashing me dirty looks. My stomach started to churn while I fought back the urge to just make a break for the truck and run.

Finally, since I could not locate a non-pregnant uterus, I astounded myself by loudly announcing that she was pregnant, and prepared for the next one. Much to my disappointment, the next one felt the same way. I was getting more nervous with each mare, making the diagnosis even harder. Making the best decisions I could, we worked our way through the dozen mares to be tested that day. I thought I was going to vomit from the feeling of total incompetence when my hand went into the last horse. Finally, the familiar skull of a foal bounced against my palm. I had just started to feel a little better about myself yelling out "pregnant" when the mare decided to get in the last word. She kicked out her back left leg with lightning speed, and her hoof cracked against my shin so hard it sounded like a shotgun blast. I reached down and rubbed it; as no bone was sticking out, I knew I could at least get to the truck.

For the first time, a smile crept across Mrs. Weber's face. Such a gesture, I noticed, was completely foreign to her tired face. She had gotten her entertainment for today and was not going to hide it. In her mind, the old mare had given me an official initiation. I'm sure it was payback for having taken so long. We said our good-byes as I limped back towards the getaway vehicle. I had never been so glad to be leaving a place in my life.

As soon as we had reached a safe distance from the barn, Jenny couldn't take it anymore and turned to me with a smirk on her face. "You had no idea what you were doing back there, did you?" she asked. I flashed her a disappointed glance. "Was it that obvious?" Jenny rolled her eyes and nodded her head. That was answer enough. Not a stellar start to the inaugural day.

My next job was a dog spay. How tough could that be? I had performed several of these in veterinary school, so I sat up straight again and guided our vehicle towards the clinic with renewed confidence.

On arrival at the clinic Jenny converted the exam room into a surgery area while I examined the patient before we got started. She was a one-year-old Doberman pinscher who appeared to be in perfect health. We lifted her onto the table, and Jenny held off the cephalic vein on the smooth front leg while I injected the inducing anesthetic into it. Like most Dobermans, she sat stoically, not even wincing as the needle penetrated her skin. When she drifted off, we placed the endotracheal tube and hooked her up to the isoflurane gas. Jenny clipped the hair away from the midline and sterilized the area with Betadine soap.

After donning gloves and a surgical mask, I opened the sterile surgery pack, eventually finding a scalpel handle, and attached a sharp new blade Standing over the sleeping dog, I made the incisions through the skin and muscle with relative ease. Then began the inevitable search for the tiny ovaries. Finding them gave me a little feeling of relief; the first steps were over. Next the ovaries were ligated with thin blue suture material, followed by the body of the uterus just in front of the cervix.

This is the point in any surgery when you hold your breath, cutting loose the tissue to remove the body of the uterus and ovaries, hoping the ligatures will hold. I slowly removed the reproductive tract from the dog, then frantically searched the abdomen for pools of blood. It looked good, just a very small amount of hemorrhage that you would expect to see after any abdominal surgery.

I began to close the muscles of the incision when a trickle of bright red blood ran out of the incision. I stopped suturing and watched it run down onto the green paper drapes that helped to keep the surgery area clean. The flow began to increase, and when I pushed down slightly on the surgery site, blood poured out onto the table and then covered my shoes. It was official—we had a bleeder! As the blood flowed out of the dog, the last bit of confidence drained from me as well.

For a moment I froze. My stomach churned and I thought I would vomit all over Jenny. A feeling of loneliness swept over me as I realized I had no professor or more experienced practitioner to turn to. The cold hand of isolation gripped me.

Finally, I realized that in order to save this animal I would have to do something very soon. With hands quivering, I removed the sutures already placed and dug back into the abdomen to hunt down the bleeder. Bright red blood was everywhere, which Jenny helped me soak up with four-by-four gauze sponges. Several times I had to bring myself back from the brink of panic, but I eventually found that the blood was oozing from the stumps of both ovaries. I had double ligated both of them, and the sutures were still holding tight, but blood still welled up from the severed vessels. We proceeded to tie off both sides with more suture material and held our breath. I could see the relief in Jenny's eyes when no new blood appeared. We had before us, at long last, a bloodless abdomen.

I closed up the abdominal muscle followed by the skin. I felt that if I closed the dog up quickly enough, I wouldn't have to know if blood was again collecting in the belly—kind of a "what you don't know won't hurt you" theory.

Jenny removed the anesthetic gas while I was closing, and the patient began to wake up quickly after the last suture was placed. She seemed a little sluggish and pale, so we decided to give her a little extra blood. If I could have, I would have given my own blood, but since that wasn't feasible we would have to look for a more realistic donor. Just outside the clinic I found Bud, the resident black Lab. He sat down at my feet, wagging his tag and smiling up at me. It was almost like he was volunteering.

Fortunately, blood typing is not required for canine blood transfusions if the recipient has never received donor blood before. We pulled a couple large syringes of blood from Bud and mixed it with some anticoagulant to keep it from clotting before getting it into the patient. I injected the life-giving fluid into our anemic patient through the I.V. catheter that Jenny had already placed. Almost immediately she seemed to perk up, and the pounding in my head began to fade away. Jenny, Bud and I kept a close eye on the young Doberman for the next couple of hours. Her gums remained pink, and by about four o'clock she began to become interested in food again.

I felt very lucky that we all survived that episode but was never really sure why she bled so much. Occasionally, Dobermans can develop a bleeding disorder very similar to that of human hemophiliacs, but the owners declined testing for this condition. We never knew for sure whether the hectic episode was due to a bleeding disorder or just the inexperience of a young veterinarian.

My first day had proved worse than your average hazing, and just when I thought it was over the phone rang. One of our hobby-farmer clients just north of town had a cow that had aborted and hadn't cleaned yet. This I could definitely handle. Removing the placenta from a cow was usually a fairly straightforward task and didn't require a whole lot of time. Dave was still out vaccinating some horses, so I knew he would be happy if I could take care of this one. Jenny had a hard day working with me, so I told her to go on home and I would be fine.

When I arrived at the Thomas farm, the cow was already in a holding chute, and a small crowd of observers had started to assemble in the open-sided shed beside her. Mr. Thomas worked at the local meat packing plant and raised cattle on the side to supplement his income. He was a tall, slender, sort of sad-looking man, about retirement age. His neighbors, for the most part, led very similar lives, and I knew they were not gathering this evening to "shoot the bull." It was time to judge the new vet in town.

I grabbed the long plastic sleeves out of the truck, heading for the business end of the cow. I grabbed the tail and moved it to the side to begin the placental extraction. My heart sank. Besides the expected placental tissues, a small, lifeless foot protruded from the cow. Worse yet, the entire area was covered with—oh, yes—maggots! I began to gag a little but held back as this would be seen as a sign of weakness, which a young veterinarian could not afford to show.

This meant I was going to need a whole new game plan. Mr. Thomas realized that the calf had not aborted after all and was staring down at his feet while kicking the dirt. His embarrassment showed, and he finally drew in a long breath to speak. "I'm sure sorry about this; you know, I really thought that calf was already out," he said in his strong Dakota accent. Then he went back to examining his shoes.

I headed for the truck to re-equip for a much bigger and more time-consuming task. I rifled through the truck, finally coming up with a pair of calf-pulling chains and a "calf jack" to help me extract what was left of the calf from its ailing mother. This piece of equipment is basically a long pole with a flat bar on one end that fits around the butt of the cow. On the pole is a lever with a pulley and a cable that, when attached to the small chains placed around the calf's legs, is used to wench the calf from the cow. I proceeded to set up this apparatus without any help from the audience.

Once the chains were in place and the cable hooked on, I began cranking the lever Eventually the cable tightened to the point of snapping, but the calf did not budge. I even tried forcing a half gallon of lube between the calf and the vaginal wall to help it slide, but the move was futile. The dead calf had bloated up over the last couple days and was now stuck like a cork. Still no helpful volunteers from the jurors. The conversation noise level was increasing, but most of them seemed to be ignoring me. I convinced myself that they were just afraid of maggots crawling up their sleeves, but in reality I think they were more like Romans in the coliseum and I was the gladiator.

Nearly an hour had passed since my arrival, and I knew that I had at least that much longer to go before winning this battle. I went back to the truck and came up with some Fetotomy wire, a thin metal fiber covered with barbs for cutting apart a dead calf within a cow for easier removal. It seems crude, but the cow would die if the decaying calf was not extracted. I delved back into my job with renewed purpose,

certain that I could extract the calf this time. But as the clock ticked by and none of the calf had been extracted from the cow, my enthusiasm started to wane.

Meanwhile, the spectators had started to regain interest in my strife. The conversation had almost come to a complete halt except for the occasional snide remarks about the amount of time that had passed since my arrival. There was beginning to be a lot of head shaking and disgusted looks. Another hour passed, and I finally had to face the fact that the calf was not coming out this way, either. With my head hung in defeat, I turned to Mr. Thomas and sheepishly admitted, "I can't get it out this way; I'm going to have to do a caesarian section."

At that point, a hush fell over the audience and a small figure wiggled to the front of the crowd. The tiny creature with a wizened face approached me. He was about 85, with a worn John Deere cap pulled down over his eyes. He used a cane to support himself since he was severely bent over at the waist from years of hard farm work. He looked up at me, raised the cane and stuck the end of it an inch away from my chest. From under the cap a voice croaked, "That's what you should've done to begin with!" The end of the cane slammed to the ground and the accuser spun around, disappearing back into the crowd.

So there I was, two hours into a job that should have been done two days before, and now I was being told how to do it. Turning my back to the agreeing nods, I went back to work once more. Within the hour, the cow was free of the calf and I was closing the incision. The spectators had dispersed except for Mr. Thomas, who thanked me for all my efforts, then headed back towards the house muttering about how long it had taken.

On arrival back at my apartment, the brand new coveralls purchased for my first day went straight into the dumpster outside. The muscles in my college-boy hands ached from wrist to fingernails, and I couldn't seem to stand up completely straight. I was asleep before the couch knew what hit it. The day that seemed like it would never come was over. I hadn't saved the world after all—just got a little beat up by it.

Always Bring Clean Clothes

Although I have never been a big-time cattle practitioner, some of the bovine calls have provided me with the most entertaining experiences of my career, and a call I got one January day was definitely among those. The middle of January in eastern South Dakota is not ideal for a veterinarian who does any large animal work. Needless to say, it was extremely cold—so cold, in fact, that the trees and bushes were encased in a white frost just from the moisture in the air. It was like driving through an enchanted forest made of fine crystal. Beautiful, but so frigid that just breathing froze the hairs in your nose.

I swung my Ford 150 pickup into the clinic driveway, hoping to have an easy morning and be able to spend most of it performing small animal surgery in the well-heated surgical room. Alas, I was greeted by the receptionist who informed me the Schmidt family had a cow that was having trouble calving. My heart sank. Fortunately, Jenny, my technician, had also just arrived, so we scooped up the appropriate equipment and headed for the truck. Jenny was quite grateful that the truck was already warmed up and hopped right in.

The full blast of the heater kept the frost off our bodies but warmed up our boots just enough to remind us of what we had stepped in the day before.

The Schmidts were a couple in their thirties and owned a little farm on the edge of town. They raised a small herd of Simmental cows and would be considered hobby farmers in most agricultural circles. They both had jobs in town, so they ran the farm in their off hours.

The heat in the truck was beginning to put me to sleep, and I almost missed the driveway. But the Dakota air knocked the sleep right out of me when I opened the door of the pickup. Jenny and I were prepared for the weather in our traditional South Dakota garb: Carhartt overalls, stocking caps and snow-ready boots. Not exactly New York runway material, yet we knew it would come in handy that day.

Mrs. Schmidt greeted us drinking a steaming cup of coffee and holding a bundled baby on her hip. "They're out there," she pointed, "but we don't have a catch pen or a head gate."

This was not good. While I've always respected people's right to own livestock, there's nothing more frustrating than needing to treat an animal and not having the proper equipment to restrain them. Chasing an upset bovine with a half-born calf in subzero weather was not the way I had hoped to spend the day.

We saw our problem standing in the far end of the pasture with two forelegs hanging from her backside. Mrs. Schmidt piped up with, "Do you think you could rope her?" Oh, why did she have to bring that up? I was terrible with a lasso, and now I would have to give it a shot. Retrieving my rope from the truck, I explained how I was not actually skilled enough to catch the cow, but I knew an attempt would be necessary to placate her.

Meanwhile, Jenny had made her way across the field and was moving the patient back in our direction. As the cow ran by, I tossed the lariat in her general direction. To all of our surprise, she literally stuck her head in the loop as she dashed by. But my jubilation quickly faded when I realized that now I had a 1,500-pound animal on the end of a rope. She realized it, too, and bolted off with me holding on for dear life. With each step and her assistance, I was suddenly taking six-foot strides, practically flying through the air. The scene must have looked like something from an old *Road Runner* cartoon. I was determined not to let go in order to try and save the calf. I knew catching the poor cow again would be practically impossible. This went on for a good 10 minutes, with me sailing behind her like a rag doll on a string.

Between gasps I yelled for Jenny, pleading with her to try and chase the cow towards one of the big corner posts on the outer fence. But rather than come running as she usually did, Jenny stood in the middle of the pasture, not moving. She just stood there like a statue even when I continued to yell for help.

At last the cow slowed and I was able to tie her off to one of the posts. After a moment of catching my breath, I slipped the calf chains around the greasy forelegs hanging from the cow and pulled with all my remaining adrenaline. Much to my surprise, the calf was still alive. His head and tongue were swollen, yet his legs began to move when I pulled. Just when I thought that I had nothing left, the glistening little fellow slid out onto the ground. Within five minutes he had shaken himself off and found his mother's udder.

Human newborns are so helpless and completely dependent on their mothers. But animals just born have no time for rest as a predator could be lurking just around the corner. A belly full of fat, rich milk and off they go. I am still in awe every time I witness a birth. So many things have to go perfectly for months to achieve a living, breathing being. I'm not sure how well Darwin's theory stands up to this kind of perfection.

I gathered my equipment, my hands now aching from the cold, and put it back in the truck, again with no help from Jenny. She just stood beside the vehicle looking forlorn. I climbed into the cab and started it up. Jenny slowly opened the passenger side door but didn't get in. She wouldn't even look at me and just stared at the ground. I couldn't hold back any longer. "What were you doing back there? I really needed your help," I told her bluntly.

Still no response, but I watched a tear roll partially down her cheek before freezing. Finally she spoke softly. "I'm sorry I didn't help, but I was laughing so hard watching you run behind that cow I … I wet my pants." Then she turned around. The seat of her coveralls was completely soaked and starting to freeze. She had been totally paralyzed with embarrassment! How could I be upset with her now?

I covered her side of the cab with old surgical towels from behind the seat and gave her a reassuring smile. We took off back into the frosty Dakota landscape, laughing about the whole crazy experience.

You Are What You Eat

Puppies are always cute and lovable no matter what breed, color or size they are. They are made this way so that someone will inevitably want to take them home. It's nature's built-in puppy marketing plan. But under that adorable fuzzy disguise can be a little monster waiting to wreak havoc. All puppies will chew on shoes and ruin socks, but occasionally you run into one who carries puppy mischief just a little too far. Often these puppies seem to mistake rocks, wood or even sanitary napkins for dog food. These diets almost always lead to vomiting and diarrhea, always on the best white carpet in the house. It was these symptoms that led to a concerned phone call on a steamy Dakota morning in late August.

The receptionist relayed the message that Mr. Ramsey had called in to say that his new Border collie puppy, Sam, was not doing well, and he needed to bring him in as soon as possible. I had just given the pup his first vaccinations the week before, and Mr. Ramsey was sure that these shots had caused the current illness. It is not uncommon for owners to blame their pet's current problem on the animal's most recent veterinary procedure. More than one phone call from a client has begun with, "You saw my dog two years ago, and now he's very sick," insinuating that whatever I did then directly caused the completely unrelated sickness that has affected the animal now. I told Mr. Ramsey to bring Sam on in and we would get to him as soon as we could.

It seemed like I had barely gotten off the phone when Mr. Ramsey burst through the door, even though he lived 10 miles away. He held an exhausted-looking Sam in his thick forearms. Even though he was 74 years old, Mr. Ramsey's body had not yet given in to time. He wasn't a tall man, but he had the wide wrists and the huge hands of a man who had carved out a living for half a century on the northern plains. He recently retired from farming, but he still wore the uniform of his trade: a white T-shirt under a pair of blue denim bib overalls with the waist buttons undone in case there was a big Midwestern meal coming up. As with most farmers who have dealt with livestock all their lives, Mr. Ramsey tried to act like the puppy didn't mean that much to him. "I wasn't that concerned about him—he's just a dog, after all, but . . the missus talked me into bringing him in." This macho image was paper thin; the concern in his creased face gave him away as he gently placed the emaciated puppy on the exam table. He explained that Sam had vomited a couple times during the middle of the night, but he was sure the pup hadn't eaten anything out of the ordinary.

Upon examination of the puppy, all I could find abnormal was some hard stool in the posterior abdomen. Since everything else turned up normal, I concluded that the little guy was just constipated, and we all know how bad that can make you feel. After injecting some electrolyte solution under his skin to keep him hydrated, I sent Sam home with some laxative tablets. Mr. Ramsey seemed happy with this treatment and thanked me heartily as he tucked Sam under his big arm to head for home. Unfortunately, I didn't share his exuberance. I had a feeling we were not out of the woods yet.

I spent the afternoon vaccinating a group of especially unappreciative young horses that required my undivided attention, realizing only at the very end of the day that we still had not heard any more about Sam. Right before the clinic closed, I called in on my truck radio to see if Mr. Ramsey had made contact. I caught the receptionist just before she made her 4:59 p.m. mad dash for the door. She informed me that in no way, shape or form had Mr. Ramsey been in touch with the clinic that afternoon and cut me off as if I was about to ruin her entire evening. I smiled as I imagined her stomping out and slamming the door at 5:01 p.m.

All evening I kept thinking about the little dog, hoping he was not getting any worse. I even had a dream that a very upset Mr. Ramsey had called in the middle of the night to tell me that Sam had died and he was going to sue me for malpractice. It was one of those nightmares when you have to sit up and look around the room for a while before you realize it was just a dream. I actually had to check in with the answering service before convincing myself that no one had paged me.

After a night of less-than-perfect sleep, I couldn't stand it any longer. The minute eight o'clock rolled around I was calling the Ramseys to check on Sam's condition Mrs. Ramsey was quick to tell me that it hadn't changed a bit. I told her that we had better get the little guy in for some tests. If she could just drop him off for the day, that would be best. She protested about leaving him at first, but after convincing her we would not perform any "scientific experiments" on Sam while he was with us, she promised to get him in. Apparently, as Mr. Ramsey explained to us later, she had recently watched a television special investigating the cosmetics industry's use of animals for laboratory testing.

That day we preformed a barium study of the puppy's digestive tract. This procedure involves a little sedative before passing a tube through the mouth into the stomach, then inserting a liquid through the tubing that will show up as white on an x-ray. Next, Jenny and I took several well-timed radiographs as the barium moved through the intestinal tract. The x-rays revealed the classic signs of blockage where the barium stopped in the large intestine and would not move past the large barrier. The mass appeared to take up the entire back half of the dog. My first thought, after examining the radiographs, was that I was just glad they weren't of my abdomen. But I was stumped, unable to decipher what made up the mass. Most often these blockages are fairly distinct on x-rays. Common intestinal plugs in puppies such as rocks, socks, and children's toys can be fun to pick out on film. But this monster was definitely something new to me. I showed it to my boss for a second opinion, but he just wrenched his face as if he were trying to pass it himself, shook his head and moved on to his next case.

Now I would have to come up with some sort of plan on my own. I knew what needed to be done next; I just couldn't face it. Then Jenny said it: *enema* Now that she had said it I would have to perform one. As I stood holding the container of soapy water with the plastic tubing attached that was now inserted into Sam's you-know-where, I felt so proud thinking of how I had spent eight years in college to become Dr. Enema. Jenny was holding the little dog's head, trying to hold back what was either a laugh or a dry heave. Finally, after several attempts at breaking up the unrelenting obstruction, I announced that allowing the soapy water to work its magic overnight would be the way to go, and Jenny called the Ramseys to come pick up their pup. Surgery would be a big risk for this emaciated puppy, so we decided to give the laxatives and enema one more chance.

I was hoping we would get a call the following morning that the concrete-like substance was in the middle of their living room floor, but no such call came. I had to look at a horse with a bellyache at a farm near the Ramseys' place, so I decided to stop in and check on Sam. Stopping in to check on a patient unannounced is always a little risky because of the possibility that they have taken the pet to another veterinarian or, much worse, the animal has passed away. In this situation I had to brush off these concerns before turning the truck down the Ramseys' mile-long driveway. I drove through the fields of six-foot-tall corn stalks forming a wall of formidable green on each side of the driveway. A yellow haze of pollen hung in front of the car, released from the pollinating tassels atop each plant. These fields were not planted by Mr. Ramsey anymore; he had sold off all of his farm except for a few couple of acres where the house sat so that he and his wife could afford to retire.

I pulled up to the modest white farm house with a huge vegetable garden on one side and clothesline heavy with overalls and bed sheets on the other. Walking slowly up the old cement steps onto the porch while holding back the urge to turn and run, I pushed the doorbell then waited. I had hoped to hear a healthy barking puppy scampering towards the door, but instead the only noise was the creaking of the porch swing beside me.

Eventually, the heavy sound of work boots moved slowly towards the door. Mr. Ramsey stood in the doorway shaking his head and made a gesture with his arm for me to come in. His facial expression gave me a clue to the situation; I was sure that little Sam was no longer. We continued into the dark living room where Mrs. Ramsey was kneeling over a fluffy dog bed, her face red from crying. She was embarrassed to be caught showing so much emotion and quickly wiped her tears with her apron when she saw me come in. I started to express my sympathy for their loss when I realized that Sam was still alive, but obviously his condition was worsening. Mrs. Ramsey spoke up: "We really appreciate all you've tried to do for him, but is there anything else we can try?"

I could not believe that the blockage had not passed yet, so I scooped up Sam and headed back for the clinic. I had one more chance to save their little companion. Speeding back out the driveway with little Sam on the seat beside me, I noticed the barrage of grasshoppers smashing against my windshield. It was one of the cyclic years in the Midwest when the grasshopper population was very high, and my increased speed had decreased their ability to clear out of my path. On the route to the clinic I re-thought the curiosity of puppies and began to develop a theory.

Back in the treatment area Jenny and I fired up the enema apparatus again with renewed hope. Once the tube was inside the dog, it was obvious the laxatives had begun to do some good; the blockage

had moved back quite a bit. We continued to flush in the fluid, and eventually a couple pieces of the blockage broke loose. Just as I surmised on my trip back to the clinic with Sam, out came grasshopper legs! Sam had not been able to resist the bouncing, brightly colored insects and felt it was his job to rid the world of all of them. We continued to break down the mass with the enema fluid, and a continuous flow of grasshopper parts emerged. By then we were both beginning to feel a little nauseous as the stench of decaying insects filled the room.

After an hour of continuous work, the last of the "Grasshopperlith" was removed, and within another hour Sam was feeling a lot better. Jenny offered him a small dog treat, which he gobbled right down. I called the elated Ramseys and told them they could pick up their little friend, but I suggested they might want to keep him inside until the grasshopper blight was over.

Mr. Ramsey soon appeared to get the pup and thanked us profusely while receiving a thorough face cleansing from the unobstructed canine. Resolving constipation will make anyone ecstatic. Mr. Ramsey happily paid his bill, made some little joke about how expensive grasshoppers were, then trotted out the door.

A few weeks later I drove past the Ramseys' farm on my way to another client's. With the corn gone by then, I could make out in the distance a slightly larger Sam chasing a bright orange butterfly through the manicured yard. I cringed automatically as the worst possible scenario came to mind. Hopefully it wouldn't be a big year for butterflies.

Holiday Pay

A big disappointment to most young veterinarians is the amount of time that is spent being on call for emergencies. Unless the practice is located near a fairly large city with an emergency clinic that will take small animal calls after hours, carrying a pager is a regular part of life. The weekends and holidays off call become a valuable commodity.

The next big surprise is what some clients feel is an emergency. All veterinarians joke about how many times a client will watch a sick or injured animal for days, only to call it in as an emergency on Sunday afternoon. And once the client has made this decision of urgency, the vet must deal with it immediately!

One of these situations happened to me on a lazy Labor Day weekend early in my practice career. I was enjoying a sunny afternoon jog on a quiet Dakota back road when my electronic leash went off. Stopping at a pay phone next to a gas station, I learned John Erickson had a lame draft horse stallion on his farm west of town, about an hour away. I told him that we would be glad to see him first thing Tuesday morning. But he replied quickly, "Ah, Doc, I was hoping you could see him today. He's been sore for about a week, don'tcha know." I gave it one more shot. "It will cost more to see him today than tomorrow," I ventured, but this didn't slow down Mr. Erickson.

Reluctantly I ran back home, checked my truck to be sure the right equipment was accounted for and headed off. The route to the farm passed by dozens of family picnics in front of big old white farmhouses with wraparound porches, yards perfectly manicured and littered with red, white and blue. It's an aspect of America that is too often left behind for amusement parks and mega-malls these days. Such family get-togethers are something I still miss about rural life.

After about an hour, I pulled in the driveway I was looking for and turned off the engine. Like the other farmsteads, it was well-groomed with the flag flying. In fact, the barn and house were in even better shape than most, but there were no picnics in this yard. Mr. Erickson was standing by the big red barn waving for me to pull the truck over closer to him. He was a tall, friendly man sporting the typical striped overalls and required seed corn cap He greeted me with a big smile and a handshake that took me a few minutes to recover from. He had the hands of a man who was not afraid of hard physical labor, even at an age when most men would have been retired. "I appreciate you coming today," he mumbled, then slapped me on the back hard enough to leave me speechless.

We headed in to see Big Mac, the delicate flower John was so concerned about. He had a sore right rear foot alright, but at 2,200 pounds, he was a little more than I was willing to grab a hold of and start poking around. We decided that a little sedative might be helpful. After all, I would be working on the business end of the horse, and it was easy to imagine him dropkicking me through the barn wall. After an injection of sedative into the monstrous animal's garden hose-diameter jugular vein, his formidable head began to drop and the pain in the hoof was temporarily forgotten. Fortunately, he was a gentle giant, and with the assistance of the tranquilizer he let me examine him without objection.

I worked quickly, trying to find a sore spot on the hoof while John patiently looked over my shoulder. Time was of the essence since the sedation would only last about 20 minutes. Finally, I found a spot in the hoof that made the big boy withdraw his leg slightly. With my hoof knife I dug into the tender area, and white pus oozed out onto the old plank floor. A pungent rotting odor immediately followed, but Mac was going to feel better very soon. Once the pressure in the abscess is released, pain relief isn't far behind. After wrapping the foot with gauze and duct-tape (yes, it works on animals too!), I gave him a big injection of long-acting antibiotic just in time for the sedation to start wearing off.

John started to become a little more talkative now that his draft horse was going to be OK We struck up a conversation while waiting for the last of Mac's hangover to wear off. He began to tell me how his wife had died a few years before after a bout with cancer, and his children had moved away in search of better jobs. His daughter lived with her family in Chicago and his son in North Carolina where he had a career in computers. You could see his disappointment that neither had stayed home to run the farm, but he understood it was a tough way to make a living in today's world.

He told me about how his parents came immigrated from Sweden and were part of a Swedish settlement near the farm. John had attended a one-room schoolhouse where classes were taught in both English and Swedish. We talked way past the time it took for Mac to wake up. He told me about his life on the farm and how it was interrupted only by the time he spent in Europe during World War II. We talked until the shadows began to get long and Mac began whinnying to get back with his mares.

John finally said, "Well, it's probably time you want to go?" I responded that I had probably better get back, and he nodded with a disappointed understanding. I waved good-bye and headed for home just as the sun tucked itself in behind the tasseled corn rows. The yards were now getting dark and the people had moved inside. Only the multicolored glow of televisions could be seen through the old four-pane windows.

I never saw John again but have thought about him often. He was from an era when we were more of an agricultural nation, when children inherited the farms and the necessary skills to run them from their parents. That period was in sharp contrast to the modern-day large, mechanized corporate farms that only require a few people to work thousands of acres.

It was sad to consider that the sun was also setting on the family farm and John's way of life. After originally having been upset about being dragged out on that holiday weekend, I realized it was a gift to be able to spend time with this man and his horse.

Watch Dogs?

I had learned growing up in rural Iowa to be wary of what might be protecting the farms and the occupants within. Usually one or more mixed-breed dogs would come running from all corners of the barnyard to converge on me when I'd visit somebody else's farm. Most achieved satisfaction just from striking fear in my heart and would commence tail wagging as soon as their mission was accomplished But others took themselves a little more seriously. Tough dogs come in all different shapes, sizes and breeds. Just because a dog looks like a kind old retriever, I've learned, the rules may change when it comes to protecting his domain.

Size can also be deceiving. I have walked to many a front door with a Yorkshire terrier attached to my ankle. With tough dogs I have learned protective tricks such as holding my hands high on my waist and not making eye contact. Looking an aggressive dog in the eye is usually perceived as an act of war that ends, for most people, in a mad dash back to the truck.

People's fear of dogs ranges from one end of the spectrum to the other. My own sister is deathly afraid of the canine species. One

Christmas break she and I were gift shopping in my hometown when we were approached by an old beagle as we came out of a clothing store. The little dog had obviously birthed more than her share of puppies as her teats nearly dragged on the sidewalk. She was making the rounds, begging for treats while her owner was solving the world's problems with his cronies on the town square. At the sight of the big brown eyes and joyful tail wags, my sister dashed back into the store as if she had seen the devil himself. It's hard to believe that we come from the same gene pool.

Normally, dogs are not a big problem when you know what you're getting into. It's when you are visiting a new client and taking that first cautious step out of the truck that things can go awry. On this particular cloudy Dakota afternoon, Jenny and I pulled into the small farm owned by Jim and Sally King. They had only owned the place for about a year, just getting it cleaned up from the previous owner who died after a long nursing home stay. They had been in the clinic with a couple of cats that required neutering, but none of us had ever been to their farm. Today we were there to see a foal with a facial laceration.

I stepped cautiously out of the truck and waited for the typical anarchy brought on by my arrival at most farms, but nothing happened. I knew that the Kings would not be home. When they set up the appointment we were warned that they would be at their day jobs in town. Jenny and I were to treat the foal in the barn, then leave them instructions and a bill on the front door. Unfortunately, they neglected to let us in on a crucial aspect of their barnyard.

Jenny and I headed towards what at one time could have been called a barn. Now it was more of a lean-to with a couple stalls and just enough siding left to slow the wind down. One of the stalls contained our young patient with her mother watching over her and eyeing us suspiciously. The little brown filly had a small cut over her right eye where she had most likely bumped her head while romping in the stall. Jenny grabbed the filly by the tail and the neck so I could inject a small amount of tranquilizer into its jugular vein. Within a minute the little horse relaxed, and I dropped down on my knees in order to get close enough to the filly's bloody head to clean up the wound. After some lidocaine injected into the skin around the injury took away the feeling, I was able to close the wound with four sutures.

Standing back up after half an hour of concentrated work, my knees were soaked with the familiar horse urine and feces that have ruined countless pairs of my jeans over the years. (My wife still gets a little frustrated when trying to find a decent pair of pants for me to wear to a social event.) The end result was a success despite my smelly knees. Except for the fish line-like sutures, it looked like the wound had never happened. Fortunately, the face usually heals well due to its good vascular supply, so the scar would be very minimal.

Little girls always ask two questions of me when their horse is injured. The first is "Will my horse be OK?" followed quickly by "Will there be a scar?" This young horse owner would be happy with both of my answers. You never know when a small blemish could keep an animal from a blue ribbon at a horse show years down the road. According to little Sara King, this new equine was destined to be a champion show animal.

While we were cleaning up I was sure I noticed something move past the spaces between the boards on the side of the old barn. I had not forgotten the lack of a canine greeting on our arrival. In fact, I had a gut feeling we were not alone the whole time we were working on the filly. As we started towards the truck I noticed another movement from behind some bales of hay stacked in the barnyard. This time Jenny noticed it also, and we agreed the quick motions resembled that of a bird. We were both becoming a little anxious when I headed for the front door to leave a note for the Kings. Jenny eased up into the truck cab and closed the door quietly. I got to the entryway, leaving a detailed note and some penicillin to give the filly for the next week.

Turning away from the door I prepared to make a beeline for the truck when I realized what had been stalking us. Three full-grown male turkeys were staring me down just five feet away. Normally, turkeys would not be that much of a concern, but these big guys appeared to have a purpose, and it seemed to involve me. Their heads stretched to chest level with large sharp beaks draped in the customary loose red skin. They reminded me more of prehistoric raptors from a Steven Spielberg movie than next year's Thanksgiving dinner. They remained statuesque until I took that uneasy first step towards the truck. This gave them the green light to attack, and they swarmed on me as if my clothes were made of bird food. I broke into a run, but they cut me off.

The three of them worked as a team, alternating their lunges. Eventually, a sharp beak drew blood from the forearm I was protecting my face with. Farmers sometimes kept a turkey to protect their sheep from dogs, but this was ridiculous. It was time to up the ante. I picked up a long stick from the ground and began swinging it in front of their ugly red heads, hoping to scare them off. But they were very determined and were not intimidated by my poor excuse for a weapon.

Meanwhile, Jenny was enjoying all the action from the safety of the passenger seat. Slowly, while wielding the stick like a sword, I made my way to the truck and jumped in when Jenny opened the door. I gulped for breath, still clutching the stick in my hands. Jenny continued to roll with laughter until I brought up the fact that the vet box was still open in the rear of the truck. Her face went immediately sober as she began begging me not to make her get out and close it. I eventually gave in, but I knew the door would still have to be closed or the medications it contained would fall out on the bumpy driveway.

There was no way I was getting out with the killer avian squawking just outside my door. Jenny pointed out that the rear window in the cab had a small sliding window. After a short struggle I popped through, crawling along the tool box until reaching the open door while the turkeys flew at me in a last attempt to kill their prey. Back in the cab I fell in behind the wheel, leaving the frustrated birds in the dust like a bad dream.

I didn't mention the incident to the Kings, figuring they already knew what monsters they kept. In fact, Jenny and I were a little too

embarrassed to tell anyone right away, but we knew one day we would
be called back out to remove the sutures. A few weeks later the call
came in and I felt anxiety creep over me, anticipating a return to Jurassic
Park. I asked the receptionist if the Kings had mentioned whether or
not they would be present this time and was elated to hear that they
would be.

Opening the truck door that next afternoon I was relieved to
see Mr. King waving at me from in front of the barn. We exchanged

greetings and I went on immediately to remove the filly's sutures. Jim nodded his approval and made a joke about my bright future in plastic surgery.

I was a little nervous as we walked to the door of the house so Mr. King could write us a check. I was having flashbacks from the previous visit and was just about to bring up the killer turkeys when I saw little Sara standing in the open doorway. She began to thank me for fixing her filly when I noticed the red marks covering her face and arms. My jaw must have dropped because Mr. King felt he needed to explain. "Those darn turkeys got her down in the front yard. It was lucky I was within earshot," he sighed. Before I could ask the next obvious question he went on to say that the big birds were the guests of honor at last Sunday's church potluck. This information gave me great confidence on my trek back to the truck. The next time we called on the King farm, I was happy to discover that they had a new Labrador puppy guarding the property.

Jail Break

One of the biggest nightmares in any veterinary clinic is having an animal escape from the facility. Every time an animal makes a break for the outside, my blood pressure goes up as I frantically hope that all the and windows are closed. Most clinics have a multitude of measures to prevent this from happening, but in our small-town mixed animal practice, it wasn't that big of a concern—until one pet changed all that.

The local bank president, James Van Meter, had a tough little dog named Bingo. James was the classic banker with a crisp, clean pinstriped suit, perfectly groomed hair and a good handshake. His dog was a cross between a Border collie and a German shepherd. Bingo had a rough start in life after being dropped off at an animal shelter as just a puppy. Sadly, he was the product of two purebred dogs whose owners were embarrassed by the impure offspring, so as quickly as possible the pups were removed from the premises. But now Bingo was the pride and joy of the Van Meter family. He was fat and sassy, as well cared for as any animal could be. His gray coat shined, and a new leather collar encircled his thick little neck.

Now he was long overdue for a little elective surgery. Men often put off neutering their male dogs. It's a macho thing, I guess; you would think we were going to do it to them.

James dropped him off on a brisk November morning, and we got to him about 11 o'clock. I collected the surgery pack and antiseptics while Jenny went to get the patient out of the kennel. When Jenny reached into the cage to retrieve him, Bingo proceeded to bite her arm. Her initial reflex was to grab the injured limb with the opposite hand, which gave the dog just the opportunity he was looking for. Evidently he had somehow realized what he was at our office for and had decided against it.

He flew from the room, making the corner just as my boss was coming in from outside. Dr. Dave swung the door open, and the pup didn't miss a stride running through it. Jenny had recovered and would have caught up with him if she hadn't slipped on the linoleum. The dog blew out the door around Dr. Dave and headed for town, just a couple of miles away. Bingo was on a mission. He stretched out to cover the maximum amount of ground with each stride, causing his body to actually become closer to the ground like a cheetah on the hunt. His ears were flat against his head to minimize wind resistance, and his tongue hung out to the side, flapping in the breeze.

Jenny and I were panic stricken. We started to follow on foot, but Bingo had a head start and there was no way that we were going to catch him that way. The thought of Bingo showing up at the bank still in possession of the parts we were supposed to remove made me cringe. Even worse, he might get hit on the road.

We looked around for something to help us capture him. Then we noticed an old fishing net hanging on the wall of the clinic garage that I had found just a few days before on the highway where it had probably fallen from someone's pickup. It had a four-foot handle and a diameter just wide enough to get around Bingo. The netting wasn't in very good shape. Some was torn too much to hold a fish but I hoped not enough for a canine to slip through. I grabbed it and we jumped in the truck The chase was on.

Jenny was driving and I was riding shotgun with the fishing net. By the time we were out the driveway she had the truck up to 40 miles per hour and was throwing gravel and dust. She was pushing 65 when we spotted Bingo in the distance, running flat out. He was in the ditch beside the road making a beeline for home. At 70 mph we were finally catching up with him.

Jenny pulled alongside Bingo, who was still at a dead run and did not appear affected by our presence. Bingo didn't even look up at us as he concentrated on his goal. Jenny pulled us just ahead of the dog, and I grabbed the net and jumped from the truck. By the time I got back to my feet Bingo blew by in the tall dry prairie grass. I made a feeble attempt with the net, but it was way too late. Within seconds I could no longer see the escapee, just the grass parting as he ran ahead of me.

Fortunately, Jenny was thinking more quickly than I was and pulled the truck about a city block ahead of our prey this time. She barely got the vehicle stopped on the shoulder before jumping out and disappearing into the sea of brown vegetation. By some miracle it came to me what she was up to, so I started running in the direction of her and the dog. I'm sure the scene of me running crouched like a Masai warrior with an old fishing net for a weapon would have made for quite a laugh down at the coffee shop. Suddenly, Jenny jumped up right in front of Bingo. He paused, stunned by her appearance, then turned in my direction. The look of disappointment on his face when he saw me just a few feet in front of him was undeniable. Could he have been capable of speech I'm sure his reaction would not have been repeatable in public. He tried to dodge to the left, but I was pumped up on adrenaline by then. With a last chance leap of faith I went for it. It was one of those times when you feel like you're in slow motion. I closed my eyes and hoped for the best. When I opened my eyes the dog was already biting at the fishing net in a last-ditch effort to regain his freedom.

Relief flowed into us as we drove Bingo back to the clinic to complete the task that we started. I was not about to take our less-than-happy captive out of the net for the ride back. He just sat on my lap and growled occasionally, attempting to bite me.

Back at the clinic an anxious Dr. Dave awaited our victorious arrival. His scowling face lit up with a broad smile when he saw the netted pooch. I'm sure he had been debating whether or not to call the liability company. This time we turned the building into Alcatraz until it was time for Bingo to go home. When James came to pick up his pet, he didn't mention anything about the incident, so nether did we. He even commented on how good Bingo looked for having such a major operation. Evidently, no one had seen our little comedy routine, so we all decided to let sleeping dogs … well, you know how it goes.

Was It Something I Said?

A few nights before my first Christmas in practice the pager went off about 6:30 p.m as I was getting ready for a date. I groaned at the realization that I would probably not be going on the date after all, and dates had been few and far between for me recently. The answering service said that Dan Meyer had called in from north of town. His daughter's horse had been caught in the barbed wire and was bleeding badly. The date was definitely off at that point.

Dan was a nice guy, just a few years older than I was at the time, with a young family. But that night he didn't have the best timing. After yanking off my dress shirt, I picked up the phone and called to cancel the date. The young woman tried to act like she understood, but she was not a big animal lover and I knew it would be the last time we would talk. So, instead of dinner and a movie, it was out into the South Dakota night.

Turning the key on my pickup, I heard the engine groan against the cold, turning over very slowly. I pressed the pedal to the floor on the second try, and the engine roared to life. I had no time to let it

warm up because the horse was bleeding badly. As I rolled out onto the interstate, the wind pounded against the truck, forcing me to keep the steering wheel turned into it. At times the gusts were so strong it was hard just keeping the tires on the pavement. The worst part was that no one else seemed to be on the road, creating a lonely, almost eerie feeling on the interstate. No one would find me tonight if I went off the road, I told myself morosely. They were all in restaurants or movie theaters, or cuddled in their homes, smart enough to stay out of this weather.

Finally, the correct exit appeared and a narrow gravel road led me to the Meyer farm. Pulling in the driveway I could see the old farmhouse in my headlights, badly in need of paint and a new porch. Beside it was the barn, or what was left of it—a skeleton of its former self. The century-old roof had fallen to the ground on one side, and a soft light came from the section that was still standing. Knowing that was where I would find the patient, I made my way through the snow towards the light.

The plan was to evaluate the situation before dragging out my weapons of choice. Inside the dusty barn stood the little mare with blood-soaked old rags wrapped around her lower right front leg. Beside the horse stood Haley, the young owner. Eyes swollen, tears frozen to her face, she looked up at me as if I were the grim reaper. Someone had already prepared her for the worst. Behind me her father stumbled in out of the storm and shook off the snow. Pulling off his cap he bellowed out, "Well, Doc, what do you think? Can you save her?" It was a question that always makes me cringe and did so especially that night since I knew I would be held to my response by young Haley. Explaining that I had not been able to take a good look yet, I proceeded to take off the saturated bandage.

Haley watched with great anticipation as the bandage slowly came off. The dried, frozen blood had solidified the rags into something that resembled a plaster cast. When I finally wedged the last of the rags loose from the leg, blood began to flow freely again. There was about a six-inch cut with a pumping artery in the middle, but no tendons or joints had been damaged. Turning towards Haley, I smiled and winked to let her know the mare would be OK. "She'll be good as new before you know it," I announced. "But it's going to take some sewing tonight and lots of re-bandaging on your part." Father and daughter both smiled, acknowledging that they could handle it.

After a couple of trips to the truck for water, suture material and bandages, the task of putting things back together began. I ligated the big bleeder and carefully closed the laceration, knowing that a minimal scar was going to be a big deal later on. Meanwhile, Haley and her dad reminisced about the ribbons that she had won at the county horse show the previous summer. Finally, I finished bandaging the leg, and they helped me carry the equipment back to the truck. As I was cleaning up the instruments, they headed for the house. Haley's dad yelled for me to come on in so we could "settle up."

Inside the modest kitchen a steaming cup of hot chocolate waited on the table, and the whole family watched as I sipped it while writing up their bill. Almost forgetting that I had been pulled away from my date, my frustration waned with the warm cocoa in my stomach and the sight of Haley's new baby sister asleep in her crib next to the heating vent.

Looking down the narrow hallway I noticed that some of the rooms were temporarily closed off so they wouldn't have to be heated. As I sat there with the young family, scribbling down the charges, I found myself leaving out a few of the items. The total ended up significantly less than it should have, but things were obviously a little tight in this household. Haley's mom wrote me a check and stuffed a Tupperware full of warm chocolate brownies into my hand.

The truck started right up this time, and I looked in the rearview mirror to see Haley waving from the lighted doorway. I was feeling pretty good about having that call behind me and thinking about heading for a little TV then bed when the unthinkable happened— the pager went off again. Since we were not equipped with cell phones yet, I pulled off at the next exit and ran into Lucky's Truck Stop. I spotted the row of pay phones they had for the truckers to use, found an open one and called the answering service. A client had called about her cat that was not using the litter box. I was telling her what to do until she could get in the next morning when I noticed that the trucker on the phone beside me was acting a little strange.

He was a tough-looking man with a lot of tattoos and a big, bushy beard, and he must have tipped the scales about a biscuit shy of 300 pounds. His dark, wide-open eyes seemed to be focused completely on me, but instead of anger they were full of fear. He slowly put down the phone and started to back away as if he had seen a ghost. Then he turned away and practically ran out the door. I looked all around me but could not figure out what he might have been so afraid of. No one else was close by. Eventually I looked down at my hands. They were covered with dried horse blood from the tips of my fingers to my elbows. I had forgotten to wash off after repairing Haley's mare. The poor man probably still believes that I had just committed mass murder, but I wonder who he thought I was talking to on the phone.

Second Opinion

An old veterinarian told me when I first became interested in veterinary medicine, "Veterinary practice is 5 percent what you know and 95 percent dealing with people." This is hard information to swallow for an aspiring veterinarian who expected that scientific information would carry him through any situation in practice. Most veterinarians, myself included, enter the field for the classic reason—because we love to work with animals. This is great, but it might be better if we could learn from the time we were kids to think, "I want to become a veterinarian because I love to work with animals and their owners." Some of the most successful practitioners I have known had good clinical and surgical abilities, but great people skills.

I learned the hard way how valuable the ability to work well with humans can be early in my career in South Dakota. A horse client of mine called about four o'clock one afternoon to see if I could help her out with a "sticky situation." A horse that was boarded at her farm was having some problems standing up, and the lady who owned the horse normally used another veterinarian. The problem was that the other vet had been called out four hours earlier but had not arrived yet. When I asked who the other vet was that had been contacted, the voice on the other end of the phone hesitated. "It's Doc Bob," she said finally. Doc Bob was almost a legend in the area. He was 75 years old and had practiced in the region his entire career. Most of the locals loved him, but younger veterinarians tended not to be big fans. He was very hard on new graduates and felt that only he was qualified to treat the local animals.

My client, Mrs. Hoye, was getting worried that the horse might die before Doc Bob arrived, so she begged me to come out and take a look. With much regret I headed out to check out the poor animal, praying that I wouldn't run into Doc Bob in the process. I let Jenny stay back at the clinic since it was so late in the day and she had indicated that she might have some plans for the evening.

The Hoyes' stable was about 10 miles away from the clinic, and I tried to make it as quick a trip as possible, hoping to be there and back before the old veterinarian showed up. I pulled into the driveway, which looked down onto the vast pasture below. In the middle of the field lay the horse on its side, and standing over the poor animal was the stooped figure of old Doc Bob. Mrs. Hoye ran up to the truck to meet me. She was a tall, attractive woman in her mid-forties. She had a kind smile that didn't fit with the cigarette that always hung from its corner. "I am so sorry, he just arrived," she said quietly, as if she was ashamed to have bothered me now that the long-awaited "master" had arrived. I was just relieved that it hadn't been me who arrived first and started to examine the animal, only to be brushed aside by my esteemed colleague.

I said my good-byes to Mrs. Hoye and began to back down the driveway when I spotted a short little arm motioning to me from the pasture. This was exactly what I was trying to avoid. He was motioning me down to assist him. My plan to escape unnoticed had failed, and now I was stuck. If I continued to pull away it would be considered rude, and I would appear not to care about the ailing horse. If I stayed I risked being made a fool of by the experienced gray-haired practitioner. Why else would he be sucking me into this situation

except to teach me a lesson, I wondered. Surely he had seen hundreds of similar cases before; besides, he was known to be an expert in all veterinary matters.

After re-parking the truck, I shuffled reluctantly towards the down horse to take my lesson in humility. Doc Bob was in the middle of explaining the reasons that he was certain the animal was afflicted with white snake root poisoning. As he ranted on I scanned the pasture for the white flowers characteristic of snake root that time of year. I would have found his diagnosis easier to swallow if there were any of these plants in the field, but I was not about to interject that thought at this point. After the dissertation was finished, he announced that it would be best if the animal was put down immediately.

By now Jamie Boyd, the patient's owner, was cradling the comatose horse's head in her lap and sobbing inconsolably. A young woman in her mid-twenties with big brown eyes, messy black hair and a face that was swollen from crying, she managed to interrupt her grief just long enough to force out, "I don't want to lose him. Isn't there anything else we can do?" Her dark eyes begged as she looked to the old veterinarian for a glint of hope. Now I was wishing that I could turn and run because I knew what was coming next. But for the sake of the animal I couldn't leave. Then Doc Bob actually acknowledged my existence. He looked at me coldly and asked the fatal question, "What do you think?" Mentioning my name would have given me too much credibility when all he wanted was for me to agree with his diagnosis and treatment.

I just stood there, trying to pick my words carefully. Mrs. Hoye caught my attention; by rising her eyebrows she hoped to encourage a second opinion. Searching for just the right words, I pointed to the two-inch cut above the horse's right eye and answered quietly, "What do you think about that?" I hoped to appear as humble as possible in insinuating that a blow to the head might have initiated the neurological symptoms.

Doc Bob scowled at me; obviously he had expected that a greenhorn would not dare to disagree with him. He quickly dismissed the

injury as having occurred after the snake root had taken effect. Yet Miss Boyd wanted desperately to try some kind of treatment, and after my thoughts were out in the open, Doc Bob could not turn back. He snapped at me, "So how would you treat him?" His impatience was becoming more apparent as he glanced back and forth between his watch and me, realizing that his supper was going to have to be microwaved.

I suggested the usual head injury treatment of corticosteroids and I.V. DMSO. He turned up his nose at the mention of the DMSO. In his words, "It makes everything smell like a garlic factory." Besides, it would take at least an hour to run in through an I.V. catheter. He stared me down as if I were the anti-Christ sent specifically to ruin his day.

Finally, the silence was interrupted by Miss Boyd's hopeful voice: "Can we try it, please?" she asked. Since it was his patient and I felt I had done enough to irritate him, I said my good-byes and made tracks for the truck. A great wave of relief began to rush over me as I felt almost ready to distance myself from this uncomfortable case.

My hand was almost on the door when I sensed that someone was on my heels. It was easy to imagine jumping in the pickup and burning rubber to escape, but I could not ignore the incessant throat clearing from Doc Bob just behind me. "What dosage of those drugs would you use?" came out as if he were giving me a test. After giving him the appropriate doses, I watched as he rooted though his truck, hesitating to analyze an occasional bottle in hopes it would be the correct one. About 10 minutes of this frantic searching had elapsed when I decided to retrieve the medications out of my truck and handed them to him. He scowled at me one more time, then scurried off towards the patient, clutching my supplies as he went.

Mrs. Hoye thanked me profusely for coming out, especially since Doc Bob had gotten there after all. "It's no problem," I grinned, and behind my smile was elation. Escape from this call without Doc Bob publicly embarrassing me was all I could ask for.

The next morning I arrived at the clinic wondering how the horse had fared. Within five minutes of walking through the door,

Mrs. Hoye was on the phone to update me. Miss Boyd was riding the horse back to her own house as we spoke, and he was doing great! It made me happy to know that the horse would be fine, yet I couldn't help but wonder how the owner perceived the legendary veterinarian now. It seemed obvious that he had slipped off his pedestal at least for a moment. I have to admit that it gave me a warm feeling to think that I might be perceived as less of an amateur by those who were present, but I was in for a surprise.

Having let the incident slip to the back of my mind and moved on with life, the whole thing came rushing back one morning a couple of months later. I had stopped to get gas at one of the local convenience stores when I noticed Miss Boyd coming out the door. Playing dumb, I asked her what had happened to her horse that evening. She looked me up and down with a tinge of disgust on her face. "Well, he's doing just fine. Hasn't missed a beat since you saw him last." Her eyes narrowed as her face moved closer to mine. Then she spoke in an almost lecturing tone: "That Doc Bob, he's a miracle worker. The absolute best. You could learn a few things from him."

It was at this point that I really understood why Doc Bob had such a viable practice: he could convince people of anything. It took me a few minutes to gather myself together and get back in the truck. As I drove off I couldn't stop thinking about the fact that Miss Boyd had been present for the whole conversation between Dr Bob and me. Wasn't she listening? Did she miss the fact that he was ready to put her horse down before I presented another option? To top it off, we never even got paid for the pharmaceuticals I had given him. I guess Miss Boyd and Doc Bob both felt I was fortunate just to have been in his presence.

Under the Big Top

Many times in life, things come up that sound like a lot more fun than they really are. One day we received a call at our clinic that the traveling circus, which had been performing in town for the last week, needed blood tests and health certificates to travel into Canada. After hearing this call come in, my employer took off in his truck for what was to be a "full day of farm stops," leaving me to do what I thought would be a lot of fun. Jenny and I loaded the truck with extra blood collection tubes and headed for the fairgrounds where the circus was set up. She was just as excited as I was. "I always wanted to get up close to the animals at the circus," she said, eyes dancing. But I wondered if it wasn't the muscle-bound, shirtless acrobat men that she really wanted to see.

We began to realize what we were in for when we pulled in behind the Big Top and no one was there to greet us. I guess we expected a welcoming committee. Egos slightly deflated, we began looking for someone to help us with the procedures or at least point us towards the animals we were to test. As we walked around the grounds looking for Hans, who had originally set up the appointment, we started sensing that the circus workers were not overly happy to see us. When we asked them where we could find Hans, they just grunted at us like New Yorkers reacting to a tourist with a map. They obviously didn't really want us there. I expect they felt that their privacy was being invaded by what probably seemed to be forced testing of their animals. As I thought about it, I realized that they had probably had veterinarians discover problems in the past that had kept them from moving on to their next destination.

Finally, after confronting at least a dozen circus folk, we found Hans, a Fabio look-alike who appeared to be in charge of all the four- and two-legged animals. His impressive stature and chiseled face demanded respect not only from employees, but also from us. He looked us up and down with an expression of disappointment. Then, after an uncomfortably long stare, he finally spoke. "Bout time you showed up. Try not to dillydally, and I want the paperwork done ASAP so we can move north!" He pointed out the locations of animals that we were to examine and strode off to his more important responsibilities.

The next thing I knew, I was trying to get blood from a full-grown elephant. At no time during veterinary school did anyone mention how to go about finding a vein on an elephant. It seemed like something one might want to do right the first time, while inflicting minimal pain. One of the handlers finally pointed out that a previous veterinarian had gotten blood from the vein in the rear leg, but he seemed to derive great amusement from my lack of knowledge before giving me this hint. The approach seemed to be satisfactory with the elephants, so we went with it and made our way down the row of giants standing in knee-deep fresh yellow straw. I breathed a sigh of relief when the last syringe of pachyderm blood was full and Jenny gently packed the tubes away. Breaking one of these sample tubes would mean coming back for more, and the patients might be a little more agitated with us the second time around.

Next we moved on to checking the camels for tuberculosis. After injecting all four of them with test material, I was able to walk away with only one face full of camel spit. We then examined the horses for any sign of contagious disease, relieved by now to see an animal we were used to dealing with. The beautiful white equine entertainers showed no abnormalities, but there was still one group of animals that I had put off until the bitter end: the Big Cats! They had five African lions and 21 tigers that needed to be checked over. I realized that I would not be listening to their hearts with my stethoscope or examining their gums for ulcers. The question was, how close did I really need to get to these man-eating felines in order to feel like I was still doing my job? The kitties were all in their individual cages, lined up in three rows—except for one that was positioned a significant distance away from the others.

The guardian of these cats was a tough-looking, 60-plus woman sitting on a stool, legs crossed, in front of the first row of cages. She had a small, thin, brown cigar hanging from her mouth and glared at me through the curling smoke that framed her face. She grunted at me in her thick Eastern-block accent, "Don't get too close; you will upset them and they have a long reach." Then she trailed off grumbling in words that were not English but were probably not complimentary either.

I now knew why my boss ran from the circus adventure. Trying not to show too much fear, I proceeded to bend over and peer into each cat's lair without stirring the animal up too much. Jenny hung back. "I'll start the paperwork," she whispered.

"Yeah, right," I thought, but at least she could call 911 if the time came. Most of the big cats just lay calmly in their cages while others growled playfully or even rolled over on their backs. I hurried down the rows and was relieved to be nearly finished when I headed for the last one in the back.

The keeper of the cats snarled something unrecognizable at me again and shook her head slowly. I later realized that she was trying to tell me, "Don't go near that one." The big tiger got one look at me and slammed his body against the cage door, pushing the limits of the latch and hinges. He let out a bloodcurdling roar and tore at me through the bars. I leaped backwards, falling into the cages behind me and thus upsetting the rest of the cats.

By the time I gathered myself back together and made sure my bodily functions had held, the Big Top felt more like a bad day on the Serengeti. I tried to leave the tent quickly with a tiny bit of dignity left, but the last of it was drowned out by the hearty laughter of the Tiger Lady.

After enjoying Jenny's recount of the day in the safety of the clinic, my employer volunteered to deliver the final test results and paperwork the next day. He just couldn't bring himself to make me go back there, no matter how funny the story may have been if I'd had to return for a second round.

Do No Harm

One of the toughest ways to make a living, in my opinion, is dairy farming. Although a number of dairies are corporate-owned and managed these days, many family-owned facilities remain across the United States. These struggling farmers are constantly dealing with the rise and fall of milk prices, feed costs and disease. Eastern South Dakota still has a fairly large concentration of these hardworking folks and their cows.

From a veterinarian's standpoint working on dairy cows can be rewarding yet exhausting at the same time. Most dairies milk the cows three times a day. This schedule keeps the cows the most comfortable while retrieving the maximum amount of milk from each one. The only problem with this schedule is that to get in three milkings, the farmers have to get started really early and finish the last one at around seven to eight o'clock at night. I found out early on that after this last milking is when they would call me if they had a problem—around eight p.m. when they went into the house. So by the time I got out of my television-watching clothes and into something appropriate for a dairy barn, I might be able to get there by nine. Depending on how far away they were it might be even later.

I also began to realize that besides being there to treat a problem, I was often the evening entertainment. After a night of "Young Veterinarian on Trial" they could catch the 10 o'clock news and go to bed satisfied. Summer was not the best time to be in a Midwestern dairy barn. They were usually kept very clean and well kempt, but it only took a little bit of spilled milk to make the whole place smell sour in the humid prairie heat.

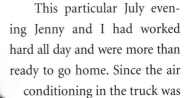

This particular July evening Jenny and I had worked hard all day and were more than ready to go home. Since the air conditioning in the truck was on the fritz, sweat had soaked through our clothes hours before. We were about a mile away from the clinic when the two-way radio crackled, "Mr. Abel has a cow down. He wants you there right away. He insists that this cow be seen tonight or he will call someone else."

Mr. Abel and his wife were in their late sixties, and their bodies had paid the price of half a century of hard work on their South Dakota farm. They both walked with a limp and were bent at the waist from stooping under the cows all these years. Tom Abel was also known as the tightest man in the county, so needless to say we didn't see them very often. The only times we did were when an animal was near death.

The red summer sun was just starting to go down behind the silos when we pulled into the rundown barnyard. The minute I opened the door of my truck we could hear the patient breathing above all the other farm noise and knew we were in trouble. The old cow was tied to the side of the barn with her front legs spread to allow for maximum air intake. I started to examine her when Tom came storming through the corral, wife in tow. "I don't want to spend a lot of money; she's my lowest producer. I don't know why I'm even messing with her," he said in his most condescending tone.

I raised up from my stethoscope just enough to acknowledge his presence, then continued to listen to her lungs. I could tell she had something blocking her windpipe, possibly a tumor or abscess. On examining her mouth I realized she may have been the oldest living cow on record and had less teeth than Mr. Abel. Finally, I stated the obvious, announcing, "She doesn't look too good"

Tom responded proudly, "The last veterinarian treated her for the same problem and she was much better by morning.

I wanted to say, "Well, why didn't you call that vet again?" but I refrained. Eventually, I came up with a plan to try to at least temporarily relieve her breathing problem.

After I explained to Mr. Able that we needed to give the old girl some I.V. antibiotics and anti-inflammatory drugs, he squinted his eyes, staring at me with detectable doubt. "She's a wild one," he said. "I don't know how you'll manage restraining her."

I suggested that we take her into the milking parlor where we could put her in a stall to keep her relatively still. But Tom informed us that she would tear up the parlor if we attempted to do this. I was running out of ideas when I happened to think that we could just lay her down with an arrangement of ropes and keep her that way long enough to give her the I.V. medication. Tom gave an approving nod to this procedure, and Jenny grabbed the cotton rope from the truck.

We easily laid her down and began the last-ditch treatment to try to save her. I was relieved to see fresh red blood bubble out of the catheter when I slid it under the skin in the general direction of the jugular vein. Attaching a bottle of medication to the catheter with plastic tubing, I held the bottle above her, allowing it to run in at the appropriate pace. After a couple minutes of time-passing conversation while the treatment continued, Jenny's elbow jabbed me in the ribs and pointed at the cow. She called my attention to a situation that I had just begun to notice. The patient had not recently moved or taken a breath. I pressed my stethoscope against the chest wall and could find no heart beat. Her gums were purple and pupils dilated. The stress of the treatment had been just enough to put her over the edge.

Mr. Abel had been spewing his opinion on the politics of the day, not noticing the stricken look on our faces. "Tom," I interrupted him, "we've lost her" He stopped in the middle of a dissertation on Reganomics and stared blankly at the dead cow. I explained that she was just in too bad of shape to survive and that I was very sorry.

All four of us stood staring at the lifeless animal for an uncomfortably long time. Finally, Tom shook his head and acknowledged that she probably would not have recovered anyway if she had died this easily. As we put our equipment back into the truck I felt that all had ended as well as it could have considering the patient didn't make it. At least she was out of her misery. We headed back to the clinic, stopping at Dairy Queen for chocolate shakes to drown our sorrows.

The next morning I stopped at the local Casey's for gas a little before eight a.m. and noticed Johnny, the owner, rushing out the door to greet me. He had a suspiciously large grin on his face as he did when he had some juicy local gossip. Today it was about me. "Hey, Doc, I hear that you killed Tom Abel's best cow," Johnny yelled across the pumps. "He said that she was fine until you got to her" Tom had already been in that morning and told him this rather imaginative version of the story. "Yeah, told me he didn't know how he would be able to stay in business without the milk produced by that invaluable cow"

I tried to melt into the pavement, but there was no escape. Johnny had a big old belly laugh over my distress before finally leaning over to whisper in my ear. "Don't worry," he said, "no one has believed anything Tom has said in over 30 years."

Rocky Mountain High

At the end of my second year of practice I decided that I could not spend another winter in the Dakotas and heard the call of the Rocky Mountains. Having spent several summers in Colorado, I missed the mountains and the outdoorsy lifestyle that goes with them.

One of those summers I worked with a veterinarian in a mixed animal practice to get some hands-on experience. We talked on the phone several times that spring, and he eventually offered me a job. It was hard to say good-bye to Jenny and the rest of the staff, but the thought of the upcoming prairie winds and horizontal snow storms made it a little easier. Winter in the upper Midwest creates a lifestyle that has many similarities to the hibernation of bears. People tend to stay in their houses and peek through their iced-up windows, wondering if the sun has forsaken them for eternity. For some reason those who grew up in the Dakotas don't seem to care. They don't mind scraping a full inch of solid ice off their car windshields every morning or the fact that all vehicles have electrical cords hanging from their engine blocks to plug them in so they'll start the next day. The leathery, creased faces of the farmers are testament to what they endure.

All this in mind, I loaded up a plywood-sided, open-topped trailer, hitched it to my 1977 Jeep Cherokee (the one that actually had the metallic Indian chief on the side) and headed southwest for Colorado. At 28 I had very little to hold me down—no serious relationships or home ownership, but no money either. This made it extra painful when my vacuum cleaner and microwave blew out of my trailer and exploded on the pavement somewhere in eastern Nebraska. With my high student loan payments and still beginning veterinarian salary, these items would not be replaced soon. No money had been put away during the previous year and a half, so by the time I reached the snowcapped peaks I was completely broke. I had just enough to make an apartment deposit and the first month's rent, but that was it. I wouldn't get my first paycheck for two weeks, and I had $20 to my name. This time was a little stressful until I discovered the Little Debbie cookies sandwich. For those who don't know, it consists of two oatmeal cookies with a kind of whipped cream in the middle. I could buy a box of one dozen for a dollar, and preparation was minimal—just open the bag. On special nights I would splurge with a side of Ramon noodles, an extra 10 cents.

My tiny cabin was very basic but came with a great view of Pikes Peak. The cabin consisted of a main floor with a rustic living room, bathroom and kitchen, and a small sleeping loft at one end that could only be accessed by a homemade wooden ladder. I learned quickly that I needed to give myself plenty of time to make it to the bathroom in the middle of the night. Excessive caffeine late in the day made for some frantic rapelling in the dark. It was tight quarters, but the beautiful views and ever-present deer in the driveway made it a great place to come home to.

I furnished the cabin with Early American lawn chairs from a local yard sale, the best I could do on my young practitioner's budget.

As you can imagine, this type of interior decorating really impressed the young ladies. Bad taste aside, with the $12 wooden-framed console television, purchased during college, it made a reasonable bachelor pad, although I did miss my vacuum and microwave. It would have been nice to warm-up my Little Debbies occasionally. When that first modest paycheck came around, I felt like a Rockefeller and headed directly for the food market.

Unlike the elaborate veterinary clinics in larger cities, rural mountain clinics tend to be rather inconspicuous, and ours was no exception. It was a small, one-story, wood-sided building that had obviously been added onto more than once. The carpet in the waiting room had been around a little too long, absorbing the odors of excrement that nervous patients had left behind. A little examination room had doors leading to an x-ray area, laboratory, and a treatment/surgery room with stainless steel kennels where patients could sleep off the anesthesia. The doctors' office was tucked in the back and equipped with a door to the outside in case a quick escape was warranted. Once outdoors, the scent of huge old ponderosa pines provided relief from any stressful events that might have occurred during the work day.

The gravel driveway ran directly from the highway about one-half the length of a city block to a four-car parking lot beside the front door. It had just enough of an uphill grade to require four-wheel drive on a snowy day. Those clients without it would have to leave their vehicles at the bottom and hike to the top. When the snow began to melt, the driveway became more of a luge course than a driveway, and it often shot clients back onto the highway a little faster than they had planned. But for all of its shortcomings, the clinic contained all that we needed to do a good job of caring for our patients and their owners.

Changing jobs not only means new surroundings, it also requires getting to know a new staff. In the veterinary profession, these people are not just fellow workers but become practically family after spending uncountable 12-hour days together. All and all, they had better be people you can get along with or those long hours will seem like years.

When I walked into work the first day, Lorraine, the receptionist, gazed at me from behind the narrow countertop that was her personal domain. At first she looked a little puzzled, then realized who I was and perked up. "Well, glad to see you could make it," were her first words. I guess I was a few minutes late. "Christie needs some help in the back." A bony finger pointed the way, and I obeyed unquestioningly. Lorraine was in her early fifties. She had sunken eyes and long dark hair with frequent streaks of gray, having obviously given up on dying it many years before. She now wore her gray locks like a badge of honor that gave her the right to dole out orders to all of us. She was the first line of defense at the clinic. Everyone and every situation had to get past her before we saw it.

In the treatment room I found my new technician/assistant covered with putrid brown diarrhea. The young Chesapeake retriever had gotten into his owner's kitchen garbage while they were sleeping. As luck would have it, the garbage contained a pot of leftover chili that had been abandoned in the fridge long enough to grow its own "shell" of greenish mold. Much to the humans' disappointment, they discovered their pup's illness while making breakfast barefoot in the kitchen that morning. The children needed a second shower before leaving for school.

Christie had made the mistake of picking up the nauseated dog to transfer it to the treatment area and had put a little too much pressure on the animal's abdomen. Projectile diarrhea on clean clothes would make most people more than a little upset, but she was obviously a dedicated caregiver and appeared to be unshaken by her soiled clothing or splattered face.

Christie was only 20 years old, but that day she looked much older than her years. Dog feces don't tend to give people a youthful appearance. She was blonde, slight of build and was rather attractive most days. Finding myself at a loss for words that morning, I mumbled out, "Anything I can do to help?" Eventually she broke a sheepish smile and wiped her hand off on her pants before jamming it out to shake mine. I hesitated, but realizing this was a test to see how squeamish the new guy was, I grabbed it and shook vigorously. "Nice to finally meet you. Can I get the name of that perfume?" I ventured.

She snickered a little and replied, "Oh, don't worry, I'm sure you'll be wearing some of your own soon enough." Then she turned on her heel and headed to the restroom to clean up. I took that chance to use the treatment room sink to wash my hands. Dog feces in the morning still make me gag a little, especially on an empty stomach.

We would later laugh repeatedly about that first meeting. There would be many days ahead when we both would find ourselves covered in horse manure, cow placenta or dog vomit. These are just hazards of the job that, when endured together, make for some great friendships.

City Slickers

Once in a while in veterinary practice you get to do something out of the ordinary and adventuresome. This beautiful Rocky Mountain fall day happened to be one of those times. A rancher client had called in right after the office opened, upset that one of the neighbor's male buffalo had gotten in with his cattle. Apparently, the bison's bravado was keeping the big boy from returning home. A group of wanna-be neighborhood cowboys had attempted a roundup, but they found the bull to be a bit more determined than their suburban mounts. Fortunately, the rancher explained, no one had died yet.

My client's fear lay, of course, in next year's crop of calves. Left too long with his cows, the buffalo would see to a new herd of "Beefalo" being delivered next spring. These were not as valuable at auction as his purebred cattle and could cause a true financial crisis for my client.

Now, where do I come in, you ask. Remember Mutual of Omaha's *Wild Kingdom*? My client requested I come quick and dart this errant buffalo with a tranquilizer so the owner could get him into a trailer. This was living! I loaded up the tranquilizer gun and eagerly hopped in the truck to head to the ranch.

A vast landscape of high, alpine pastures and groups of evergreens opened up before me. The ranch had been in this family for generations, tucked away in a remote region served by the practice. I shook myself free of the visions of playing Jim, the Marlin Perkins sidekick, with my body half out of a speeding Land Rover aiming at an angry Cape buffalo.

The large sign as I turned off the dusty road read "Kugler Purebred Hereford Ranch." Another sign with a "K" set on rockers, revealing the family's Rocking K Ranch brand, hung at the ranch entrance. A cattle guard shook the truck cab as I pulled up to the house. The dust cloud I created temporarily obscured a motley-looking crew of greenhorn ranch hands who appeared to be discouraged.

I had barely unfolded myself out of the truck when I was met by the owner of the buffalo. Mr. Seldon was a tall, disheveled man with deep-set eyes. I didn't know him personally but had heard he transplanted himself here from New York 20 years earlier with the dream of raising buffalo. He briefly glanced my way and then grunted, "I don't want you to hurt him—just slow him down a bit." Over his shoulder a 2,000-pound bull bison appeared in the distance. From my vantage point, he looked like an army tank with horns, and my last concern was my hurting him.

The plan conceived before my arrival was to drive the big boy past a broken-down shed that I would be hiding in. At the precise moment, I would take aim and hit him with the dart. Precision was the key. I had to load the dart with just the right amount of drug. Too little would just make him mad, and too much might kill him. If I missed—well, that just wasn't an option.

I watched the "cowboys" begin to gather, sporting their lassos and appearing intent on using them. I warned them that if they agitated the bull by throwing the ropes too soon, the sedation would have a reverse effect. They nodded in slow agreement. I preferred they simply walk behind him after the sedation took effect and gently coax him towards the trailer. They did not nod their heads in agreement with this. What kind of a macho war story ended with "and as we coaxed him to the trailer . . ." No! They imagined dragging the beast in victory. I couldn't allow them to get hurt. I imagined my vet school classmates shaking their heads in shock and disapproval as they read about it in the monthly liability reports in the veterinary journals. It was time to commence with the plan. I knelt in the shed and waited for the cattle to amble by. I have to admit that I may have briefly imagined myself in a fringed buckskin jacket, ready to fell a buffalo to bring back to the hungry pioneers. Back to reality, though, there he was, just 20 feet away, slowly following the cows. I second-guessed my sedation dose. Was it too much? Not enough? It was too late now. I peered through the crosshairs and pulled the trigger as he came into view. I heard the low *thump* of the dart hitting the tough hide and saw his agitated kick A direct hit! I almost went into a touchdown dance but decided to act as if I expected no other outcome. Everything was going according to plan. Our shaggy friend began to slow and get wobbly as if he'd had one too many martinis. Within a minute the great beast lay down, and I began to pack up and head to the truck. My work here was done. Quick, precise, and clean. The whole episode went off like a perfectly executed fourth-down play.

Suddenly, a roar went up from the cowboy crowd. Yes, one of them had thrown a rope on the bull, yanking him back into reality. Throwing the rope around the fading animal's neck caused him to spring up and tear off into the woods with the rope dragging behind.

I felt I couldn't leave the situation until the animal was again subdued. I grabbed a second lasso out of the truck and headed for the woods with no particular plan—just complete agitation with the now-sheepish-looking group of "helpers." The bull was up and running but still a little sedated. The idea came to me that I could tie my rope to the one he was already wearing and possibly recapture him. Running through the pine trees after him I must have looked like an idiot. But he eventually slowed just enough for me to grab the end of his rope. Using some Boy Scout ingenuity I lashed the two ends together in a square knot while keeping pace with the fleeing beast. This left a long enough expanse to tie him off to a tree, not taking into consideration what he would do when he hit the end of his new leash.

In a split second he hit the end of the rope, and it stretched like a bungee cord. The tree groaned under the tension, but the hundred-year-old roots held fast. At this point, my worst fears were realized. He began to turn towards me and lower his head. I was almost too tired to care until he began to charge. I sprinted away from him, grabbed my tranquilizer gun, and headed for the truck. He was right on my heals when he ran out of rope for the second time. Now my work here was truly done. Speeding away, I waved and yelled a hearty "good luck!" out the window.

Over the next couple of weeks, I wondered what had happened to the buffalo and his handlers after I vacated the ranch. Then, one morning I was heading towards the bank when Mr. Seldon came out of the building. He was walking with a limp that I didn't remember him having before, and his left hand was wrapped in a bandage. He waved when he saw me "Hey, Doc, thanks for all your help with that bison. We got him home safe and sound." Then he slid into his old truck and took off. I didn't have the heart to ask how he got the injuries, but since we hadn't received any calls from attorneys I felt it was best not to know.

Seemed Like a Good Idea

"We also glory in tribulations, knowing that tribulation produces perseverance, and perseverance, character; and character, hope."
— ROMANS 5:3-4

Animals so often display traits that I truly admire. Ignoring the force of terrifying foes they press on, denying their battle-weary bodies rest until the job is done. Animals can be extremely tenacious, especially when it comes to taking on other beasts. For some reason porcupines seem to bring out this "never give in" attitude in their opponents more than any other species.

How many times have I witnessed the results of canine-versus-porcupine encounters and ended up treating them? Cats rarely end up in this predicament since they are usually smart enough not to make such a painful mistake.

Contrary to popular opinion porcupines don't "shoot" quills at everything that moves. In fact, in order for a quill to find itself in another being, the potential predator has to make contact with the porcupine. These spike-covered creatures move very slowly, like a drunk who takes every step with concentration and deliberation. They are not really capable of running, so when attacked they just curl up in a ball as if to dare predators to take a bite. Any animal naive enough to try to eat them will end up with a face full of quills. Man's best friend seems to be the most common animal to fall into this category.

The most pitiful porcupine victim I have ever treated had 500 quills carpeting the roof of its mouth as well as its nose and paws. After a couple hours of surgery, the dog was quill-free, but he visited me 11 more times for repeat offenses over the next few years. It is just a myth that dogs learn from such a miserable experience.

My favorite victims of a porcupine's wrath were three Jack Russell terriers who hailed from a remote mountain area called "the park" about an hour from the clinic. The Jack Russell is the definition of a big dog in a little-dog suit. They all behave as if someone forgot to tell them they are small. On a summer Sunday afternoon about one o'clock Mrs. Conner, the owner of these three Jack terriers, called in a panic because the entire crew had attacked a porcupine. She was leaving immediately, bound for the clinic.

Mrs. Conner was a small but determined woman of about 45. She seemed a perfect match for the canine breed she had selected as pets. When they arrived, the three musketeers were pretty proud of themselves. Each one had about 20 well-placed spikes in the end of its nose and came prancing in as if the quills were trophies.

"I can't believe *all three* found so many quills!" Mrs. Conner exclaimed. Then, to her dogs, she added, "There are easier ways to attract attention to yourself, you know!"

One by one they lined up proudly, practically refusing sedation. Each one stood like a statue on the exam table, too macho to show pain, until they finally sat, sedated. Mrs. Conner held them and soothed them while I worked. Her slight hands made the magisterial terriers look, and probably feel, much bigger than they really were.

Slowly, every quill was removed from the now-sleepy hounds with a quick tug. The dogs were given back to their owner, no worse

for the wear. Within minutes, they were harassing the clinic cats. I sent them home with sore noses and antibiotics. I finally returned to my basement apartment to finish my Hungry Man meal and catch a Sunday afternoon nap.

A little after four o'clock my pager went off, and I sleepily fumbled for the phone. It was Mrs. Conner again, but this time she had frustration, not fear, in her voice. Through clenched teeth she seethed, "They finished him off this time, and I'm on the way back in!" *Slam* went the phone in my ear. An hour later I gave her a wide berth as she flew through the familiar clinic doorway. Under both arms were tucked three exuberant terriers, faces completely full of the silvery spikes this time. Evidently, these dogs had taken out a little vengeance on their porcupine friend, and they were again proud of the results.

General anesthesia was required for removing this many quills, so it was a couple of hours before they were once again released to their exasperated owner. Mrs. Conner glared at the bill, then turned to her groggy little friends. "So how do you plan to pay for this?" she asked them sternly. They responded with only somnolent smiles and wagging tongues, eagerly awaiting their next adventure even in their dreams. I heard later that the terriers spent the next two weeks "grounded" in the garage.

Occupational Hazard

Veterinary practice can be a dangerous endeavor. There is always the risk of dog and cat bites, which may be induced either by fear or pain that your treatment might cause them. Although these wounds are sometimes very painful and may produce a lot of veterinarian blood, they are not often life threatening. It is the large animal side of practice that can require an increase in life insurance. I have been chased by a multitude of cows, spitting llamas and even an occasional upset sheep, but the horse probably has been the animal to come closest to ending my career.

I have always had a great fondness for horses, and we were lucky enough to have them as pets growing up, starting with dear old Midge, the wonderful Welsh pony These early experiences allowed me to develop a huge amount of respect for these beautiful, powerful creatures. It is amazing to reflect on the role they played in developing civilization up until just the last 100 years. We humans could never have done it without them, but most of them are now relegated to the position of pets and recreation. Unfortunately, since we live in a society that no longer requires the daily use of horses, not only are horse owners able to spend less time with their steeds, but some horse owners are not well equipped to deal with these animals. Most of my clients do a great job of training and caring for their equine companions, making my dealings with them an enjoyable experience, but every so often a horse comes along that is less than pleased to see me.

A prime example of unruly patients occurred on a brisk Colorado spring day when I headed out to see a new horse client. Calling on familiar clients you know what you're getting into with both the horses and the humans, but this was not the case that day. As I stopped the truck in front of the typical cedar-sided mountain home, a small-framed, smiling woman of about 35 with long dark hair and cowboy boots came up from the barn. She stuck out her hand and introduced herself as Jane Scott, a newcomer in the community. She appeared to be genuinely happy to meet another resident of the county and introduced the two grade school-age children peering shyly at me from behind her. After a lame attempt at making friends with the youngsters, I loaded up with vaccine and followed the group towards the stable. They had five horses total, four in neat, clean stalls and an especially large one pacing nervously in a high-fenced round pen outside. Jane suggested that we take care of the stalled horses first, so I took her advice and we headed into the barn. The patients were four beautiful, well-mannered quarter horses, all standing perfectly still while I examined and vaccinated them. I seemed to notice Jane becoming a little nervous as we finished up with the last shiny, freshly groomed animal. I gathered up my supplies and we headed back outside to complete the task.

The children, who had seemed to enjoy observing the shots their pets had to endure in the barn, now made a break for the house, disappearing inside through the back door. It was about this same time I noticed that the buckskin horse we were approaching was not diligently well-groomed like the other horses. In fact, he was rather shaggy and unkempt. As we approached, Jane's pace slowed until she stopped in front of the pen and we both stared at the big horse in front of us.

She looked down at her feet, kicking the dust as she spoke "I always meant to have him gelded but never really got around to it," she said. She went on to tell me that "Rebel" was now nine years old and hadn't been worked with much. Jane indicated that they just hadn't had the time to spend with him, but I was beginning to surmise that he might not be that easy to be around. A nine-year-old untrained stallion was going to be a formidable patient.

Jane was trying to hide her tremors as I followed her into the corral. "I really need to get him vaccinated; it's been a couple years," she said sheepishly. Then she added reluctantly, "The last vet wouldn't come back" Her dark eyes glanced in my direction to look for a reaction.

I knew that I could not show fear because both she and the horse were looking for any sign of weakness. The big guy snorted and shook his head as we entered his domain. I swallowed hard when the heavy metal gate slammed closed behind me; now we were committed, or so I thought. Jane stood on her tip toes. She clipped the lead rope onto the halter and handed it to me so Rebel and I could get acquainted before we attempted any vaccinations. Talking softy, I attempted to move in closer to gain his trust. "Easy, big guy, lets take it easy," I whispered while trying not to falter.

He stared me down for a moment, then blew out all the air from his lungs through his nasal passages, producing a startling snort and nearly knocking off my hat. Jane's anxiety seemed to increase even more, and she kept looking around as if hoping to locate an escape route. It was officially a standoff. The next move was mine, so I reached into my pocket and drew out my stethoscope. With the ear pieces in place I moved in to listen to his heart, but Rebel took this as an act of aggression and stood up on his back legs, striking out at us with his front hooves. I dodged to the side just in time to see Jane slide under the fence and sprint for the deck on the rear of the house. Upon reaching her destination she turned and yelled back, gasping for breath at the same time, "I think he'll be better without me in there"

Now it was just me and the 1,300-pound, testosterone-filled equine. I decided to assume that his heart and lungs were fine and go right for the shots. He seemed to be all muscle and hooves as he bucked and charged around the pen after recognizing the syringes I pulled out of my pocket. I managed to keep a hold of the lead rope even though he would charge me, teeth bared, every 30 seconds. What I really wanted to do was follow Jane's lead and make a mad dash for the safety of the house. But I had to stay and get the job done. I couldn't show weakness, especially in front of a new client. It was one of those moments when I felt like the rest of the world had fallen away and all that existed was the horse and me.

Trying to accept that I would most likely be killed by this upset animal, I just let him continue circling around me. Much to my surprise he eventually began to slow down. The big horse was beginning to wear out. Finally, the stallion came to a stop and turned to face me, but this time he didn't attempt to charge; he just stood quietly, covered with sweat. His eyes were focused directly on me, yet the anger was gone and a soft look of submission had replaced it. I moved towards him cautiously, waiting for an explosion of teeth and hooves. Again I was surprised that it didn't happen, even when I produced the syringes again. Rebel let me rub him on the side of his neck with the palm of my hand and assure him quietly as the needles found their target in the large muscles of the neck. At last he was vaccinated, and he even let me check his teeth, heart and lungs without objection.

Jane had her hand covering her eyes while peeking between the fingers as if she were watching a scene in a scary movie that she didn't want to look at but couldn't resist. I'm sure she didn't think I would live through it. After taking off the halter I handed it to her and we settled up. She seemed happy to pay it since Rebel actually got his vaccines this time, and I was just glad to have survived. In fact, I had a little fantasy about seeing a moving van in front of their house before vaccination time the following spring.

As lucky as I was not to have been damaged this time, my next encounter with an upset equine would not have such a happy ending.

The next couple weeks of spring vaccinations went by without incident. All the horses were cooperative and well-mannered, but a

call came in on a Monday morning that would change all that. It was from a family that lived on about 80 acres surrounded by national forest. I was never really sure what they did for a living, yet they seemed to get by and still be able to afford a few horses. A certain population of people in the Rocky Mountains have an uncanny knack for being able to maintain their lives without actually going to work every day, and the Linns were among them.

Mr. Linn was a tall, Abe Lincoln type whose fashion statement never varied from a once-white T-shirt and a never-ending supply of dirty jeans. Much to my dismay, his wife was always impeccably dressed in what seemed to be the latest New York fashions. They made a unique pair with her standing beside her shabby husband in her little black dress and designer shoes. They lived in a very modern log home on a little ranch, which would have been hard to maintain on the income from Mr. Linn's wood cutting income. It was rumored that his wife was from a wealthy East Coast family and had moved to Colorado to find herself a mountain man. I would not doubt the validity of this gossip after observing her new Mercedes parked beside her husband's vintage pickup. However, I was invited there that day not to make judgments about their lifestyle, but to check out a young horse that had had a hard weekend.

They had invited some friends up from the city for the weekend for relaxation and horseback riding. Things were going well until the Linns asked their company to fetch one of the horses up that was hiding in the pine trees about a mile from the house since he would be needed if everyone was to have a mount. As the Linns explained it, Mr. Jeske, who was decked in shorts, black socks and Rockports, directed his family to head out with pocketfuls of horse treats to entice the animal But instead of riding another horse out to find the missing creature, they opted to round him up with their late-model, oversized SUV. Amazingly, they returned an hour later with the horse. Unfortunately, they had brought him back tied to the rear bumper of the vehicle. As you can imagine, this made for a less-than-happy animal. The Linns immediately realized that they should have given more detailed instructions for equine retrieval, but it was too late by then. Besides the mental damage the horse had a few scrapes and small cuts that would need veterinary attention.

On my arrival I found an extremely agitated patient who was not pleased to see another human appearing on the scene. He snorted and violently pulled back against the tree he was now tried to. His nostrils were flaring and he pawed the dirt, exposing roots that had never before seen daylight. It would take years on the couch to fix this one.

He wasn't a huge horse but made up for size with quickness and tenacity. I didn't like the situation, yet wounds would have to be clipped and cleaned before I could leave. I retrieved a syringe full of sedation from the truck and went about the process of trying to insert the needle into the jugular vein in the horse's muscular, sweaty neck. As might be expected, the horse did not think that he needed to be sedated and proceeded to strike out with his front feet whenever I got near him with the syringe. If I attempted to come in from the rear he would kick out at me with both back feet. It was hard to blame him for not trusting humans after his ordeal behind the car, but it didn't change the fact that I needed to proceed with the treatment. After about 20 minutes, he decided to let me in close enough to gain access to the target area. The needle found its mark, and my thumb forced the plunger in with panic speed. In a few minutes the medicine started to take effect, causing him to stumble a little as if he'd had one too many. This was my cue to grab my clippers and get started with the treatment.

Usually a tranquilized equine would not be bothered by the quiet humming of the cordless handheld clippers, but this particular steed was still hypersensitive after the incident and sprang back to complete consciousness as I began to work. He managed to rear up, placing his right knee between my legs as he went. It is not hard to imagine which of my body parts the knee connected with. I found myself lying on the ground eight feet away from where I had been standing a half second before. An unearthly pain began to crawl up my pelvis and abdomen. It was the same sensation I remember having on the playground when one of my classmates missed the soccer ball and landed his foot in my crouch instead, except this blow came from a 900-pound horse, not a 100-pound sixth grader. The effect was tenfold, causing me to writhe on rough, decomposed granite in the fetal position.

The clippers I was holding had flown out of my hand and hit a nearby tree, fracturing into multiple pieces. As I began to regain my senses it became apparent that Mr. Linn was fighting with the horse to keep him from coming after me again. His ears were pressed flat against the back of his head, his teeth bared and the conjunctiva around his eyes bright red with anger. It was hard to believe that the animal had such a vendetta for me, but he was just determined that another human wasn't going to mess with him again.

Working to hold onto a thread of dignity, I was able to get to my feet. Still doubled over and walking very stiffly, I gathered up the remains of my clippers with the hope of salvaging some functional parts. The truck seemed like miles away, but I was able to get to it at a snail's pace. Clinging to it for support, I dug out some ointment for the Linns to apply to the horse's wounds themselves and some antibiotic powder to put in his food. I managed to drive home feeling every bump along the way as if it were a land mine.

After two days I could finally stand up almost straight and had worked up the courage to go back to work, loaded up on Advil. Unfortunately, most small veterinary clinics don't offer sick or personal days; besides, I didn't want to have to explain to a lot of clients which injured body part was causing me to miss work. The next couple of weeks I was definitely more cautious on horse calls.

Since then, trying to stay out of the line of fire while keeping my thighs close together has prevented a repeat performance, but every time I see that crazed, wild-eyed look in a horse, this experience replays in my brain. It only takes a split second for an animal this large to do irreparable damage to a human being. I was lucky to get off with just a warning and not a disabling injury. It's natural for frightened animals to protect themselves, and you can't blame them for doing so. But I have to say that this rationale doesn't make it hurt any less.

Taking the Bait

Sometimes we humans are not the most intelligent creatures, and occasionally we even involve animals in our stupidity. In veterinary practice it seems like these lapses in judgment occur most on holiday weekends. Here in the West, people who live anywhere within a 10-hour radius of the mountains will load up every possession they might need for a lunar landing, dust off the camper trailer and head for the high country. Unfortunately, the list of essential camping gear often involves an unsuspecting pet. I always dread these weekends because animals from the suburban environment so often seem to find trouble in the mountains.

One particular Saturday morning of a Fourth of July weekend, we got a call from a beer, bait and gas shop in a lake resort area about 20 miles from the clinic. The lake, a tranquil body of water surrounded by shimmering peaks, is usually a haven for wildlife and the occasional local fisherman, but on summer weekends it is transformed into a refugee camp. I have often wondered how much fun it can be to "get away" to a place where one family is practically on top of another. It seems a lot like some of the neighborhoods the people are escaping from. I heard Lorraine, our receptionist, sigh as she got off the phone that morning: "Tourists! They've had some trouble with their cat and are on their way in. They were so upset that was all the information I could get out of them."

After the phone call we continued to see our scheduled appointments. Saturday mornings in veterinary clinics are always a little crazy because most people are off work and have time to bring in their pets. As expected, we already had a full waiting room that morning. The white plastic chairs that lined the walls were all occupied with impatient clients. An older man held a thin, gray miniature poodle whose breath desecrated the entire room, as if something had died in its mouth. A teenage girl sat with an immense mastiff at her feet, sprawled on the yellow linoleum. Duke, the mastiff, was in for his biannual toenail trim, which always involved several helpers and looked something like a professional wrestling extravaganza. Another woman sat in the corner clutching her terrified cat, who would periodically retch as if trying to vomit, yet nothing came out. I was certain that at any minute a hairball would eject from the feline's mouth and shoot across the room. The other seats were taken by those in need of routine vaccinations and examinations.

I was in the middle of explaining canine dental care to the fire-breathing poodle's owner when our injured cat and his owners burst through the door. The wounded cat had not fallen prey to any creature of the forest, but presented with a long strand of fishing line hanging from his mouth and a look of terror in his eyes. The young couple that the cat belonged to had for some reason decided to take the pet fishing for the weekend. Usually members of the feline species are not considered the best companions for outdoor activities, preferring the plush surroundings of home or a dog-proof yard. I don't know if these relative newlyweds felt bad about leaving the cat at home or if it substituted for the child they did not have yet. Whatever the reason, it turned out to be a less-than-perfect plan.

The Shaws looked to be about 28 and not very much like the outdoorsy type. Brad was a little doughy and pale, wearing a pair of Hawaiian shorts and a T-shirt with the Greek letters of a fraternity on the front. His wife, Brenda, had white skin that shined and reeked of sunscreen. She hardly seemed old enough to be married yet appeared to be the "chief" of this family unit. "Please help us—we called ahead," she choked out between breaths. I wanted to make a joke about having held a table for three but deemed this not to be the appropriate time, given their frightened looks. The little cat was completely freaked out.

Brenda quickly explained that they had been using bright red salmon eggs for fishing bait, and when Brad drew back to cast, Socks could not resist swallowing the entire bait and hook. The round red eggs dangling at the end of a fishing line must have looked to Socks like an elaborate cat toy. " We tried to get it out," she cried, "but Socks freaked." So they had cut the line free and headed our way with the hook still inside the cat.

Driving for 30 minutes with Socks attempting to get air in past a fish hook was like being in a cage with a grizzly bear. Brad had taken the brunt of the attack. He had the task of holding the frightened feline on the trip in. His thighs and hands looked like they had been through a paper shredder. Blood seeped from the multitude of bite wounds, and his hands had begun to swell.

I grabbed the cat away from Brad's stiff hands and placed him on the exam table. Christie already had a syringe full of anesthesia drawn up and slid it into the muscle of Socks' rear leg. The injection was unnoticed by the cat whose focus was completely on the pesky fish hook. In just a few minutes sleep overwhelmed him, finally bringing peace to the entire office. The anesthesia allowed us to get a small hemostat through the cat's mouth and down to the hook. With some gentle twisting the hook came loose, and Socks could breath easy again. He received an anti-inflammatory injection to reduce the swelling in the throat, and Christie placed him in a recovery cage in the back. The short-acting anesthetic quickly wore off, and the feline soon acted as if nothing had happened.

Within an hour Socks was purring and looking for food. The humans, unfortunately, were not faring as well. By the time I walked back into the waiting room to give them the good news about Socks, Brad's hands looked like catchers' mitts. The signs indicated infection was beginning to brew. Cats normally carry a lot of bacteria on their teeth and claws, so unsuspecting victims almost always end up with an infection. Left untreated, these situations can even be fatal.

We instructed Brad that he had to see a physician immediately, but like most of us men he went the macho route, brushing off his condition as "no big deal." Finally, after much nagging by Brenda and me, in addition to even more swelling, he caved in. They collected a much-relieved Socks, paid the bill, and headed for a local M.D. I was sure this time the story of how the injuries came about would be even more embarrassing for the beleaguered couple.

After they left we went on with the day, working through the rest of our Saturday patients and trying to resist the urge to make "catfish" jokes.

Miniature Menace

Animals, like people, should never be underestimated due to their size. Some of the toughest dogs I've dealt with have weighed under 30 pounds. And the average 10-pound cat can wreak havoc if asked to do something that might seem even slightly inappropriate in feline society. But Jefferson, a Sicilian donkey, has been a standout in my career as a representative of the small-but-mighty crowd. Sicilian donkeys are actually a miniature version of their larger counterparts with which most of us are familiar. Like the rest of the occupants of the island for which they are named, these long-eared Sicilians are not to be slighted. The little burros are very cute at first glance. They have a gray or black wiry coat and tiny dark hooves as hard as graphite. They usually stand about two and a half feet at the shoulder but are dominated by a huge set of fuzzy sound detectors. Not many predators are quiet enough to sneak into their space without being noticed.

My neighbor has an unneutered male, but someone forgot to tell him that he's a miniature. He struts around the horses that he shares the pasture with as if he were Big Man on Campus, and he has a set of lungs that Pavarotti would be proud of. Every day when my neighbor turns on the house lights at 5:30 a.m. the little fellow lets go, braying at least 10 times, reminding his owner that he will need to be fed soon and acting as an alarm clock for the entire neighborhood in the process. Fortunately, on weekends my neighbor tends to sleep in, not flipping the lights on until seven. After hearing the early morning wake-up call, people are always taken aback when they actually meet the perpetrator. They expect a beast that can at least look over the top wire on the fence.

My client Jefferson was not much different from my neighbor's donkey—maybe even a little more belligerent and cocky. He also lived with a pasture full of horses and filled the role of leader whenever the opportunity arose. His owners may have spoiled him just a little as he had gotten very hard to handle over the previous couple of years. He would hear my truck pull in the driveway and begin to plan his getaway. Even when it came to vaccinations or routine treatments, he would have to be practically lashed to a post just to slow him down long enough to accomplish my task.

Jefferson led a life of significant excess, and his diet had never been restricted. Out of love he had been fed a regular diet of horse treats and carrots on top of his normal hay rations, and as a consequence he had become nearly as wide as he was tall In fact, his back had gotten so wide you could have easily served a meal for four on it. I talked to the Murphys many times about Jefferson's weight issues, but Mrs. Murphy could never resist his sad brown eyes and the long, batting lashes. All she ever said was, "He's just so darn cute, I can't deprive him of anything."

Although I was never sure who owned whom, Mrs. Murphy clearly loved Jefferson. She was a cheery 40-year-old who was always in great physical condition. She rode her mountain bike religiously every day and ate only the healthiest of foods Yet, none of these habits seemed to trickle down to Jefferson. I always wanted to suggest she take him with her on a few bike rides but couldn't quite get myself to bring it up. His attitude also showed some parallels to that of a spoiled child who always gets what he or she wants. Jefferson was never forced to do anything he didn't want to. But the day of this visit I finally decided I would have to change that mindset.

I was called because Jefferson had a front leg full of porcupine quills where he had attempted to stomp on the small but well-protected animal. The quills would migrate into Jefferson's tendons and joints if not removed rather quickly. With Mrs. Murphy gone for this mid-summer weekend, her husband, Don, and I were left to talk Jefferson into the procedure. Luckily, Don was a strong fellow who was in good shape because Jefferson and his comrades had full run of a 20-acre pasture with no barn or catch pen to coax him into. This meant that we would have to corner the little monster and get a halter on him.

I knew that this was going to be a much larger job than it might have seemed to the casual observer, especially with Jefferson's buddy and bodyguard protecting him. A big sorrel draft horse named Ed had decided that his position in life was to watch over Jefferson, keeping him safe from husbands and veterinarians. The little donkey would run in and out of Ed's legs as they moved across the field together. If we got too close, Ed would lay back his ears and bare his teeth to keep us at bay. Finally, Jefferson made a wrong step, allowing Don to get between him and Ed. Working together we drove the tough little guy into an area where the sides of the fence came together forming a corner. We moved in slowly while Jefferson nervously tried to find an escape route, attempting to dart past us as his world got smaller bit by bit We almost had him when he decided that I was the weakest link and made his move to run past me. I stuck out my arm with the intention of hooking him in the crook of my elbow, but I had drastically underestimated him. Jefferson had played this game before and became airborne just as his chest connected with my arm. From afar the scene must have unfolded like an old cartoon. He knocked my 235 pounds easily onto the ground and stormed away. It

was not a stretch to believe he was laughing at me with his head held high as he returned to his comrades. Don was laughing, too. "Doc," he said, "he ran you over as if you weren't even there. It's a good thing he's only a miniature."

If there was any doubt what we were up to before, the donkey had now broken the code and the secret was out. The second try would be even harder. By the time Don and I had caught our breath and gathered some strength back, Jefferson was hiding directly under his guardian. Ed's tree-trunk legs stood like pillars to hold back intruders. After 20 more minutes of darting, dodging and near death experiences with Ed, we got them apart again. With Jefferson back in the corner, we began to close the trap once more. This attempt would have to be different because both humans were starting to lose steam while our prey was no worse for the wear.

I have to admit to feeling great relief when the determined little donkey turned towards Don and made a run for it. Learning from my shortcomings Don decided to go for a tackle. But this was no high school football player from a quarter century ago, and there were no penalties for use of teeth or hoof. I'll give Don credit for agility and strength, but not for self-preservation. He got a hold of the quill carrying running back and was dragged well past the goal line. Still holding on for dear life, Don somehow managed to get Jefferson onto his side. I came sprinting in from the side with a halter and jumped onto the pile.

Just after Jefferson was on the ground he began to thrash Don relentlessly with both back legs. As I struggled with the halter, I could see Don's face redden and grimace from the pain. Then, as I was about to fasten the halter in place, I felt a crushing pain in my left hand. No, it wasn't a heart attack—my entire hand was in Jefferson's mouth, and his incisors were clamped down on it like a vice. I managed to yank it out of his grip, tearing the skin as I did. Warm blood ran down my arm, and I was about to give in when I realized Don was still taking a beating. As I finished my job of locking the halter on tight, Don and I let our patient up and gasped for breath, both of us bent over with our hands on our knees sucking at the thin mountain air for its precious oxygen.

Jefferson let us recover in the spirit of fair play, but when I pulled out the hemostats for quill removal, he tried another break for safety. No way we would let him go this time. Don held onto the lead rope and I went for the quills, removing them quickly as Jefferson reared and kicked. Fortunately, I was used to moving targets during this type of procedure, and it was over in minutes. I might have been disappointed if he had not taken that last shot at us with both back legs when we let him go. I like to think it was his version of a thank-you, but I'm afraid he meant something a little different. At least the quills were no longer in his leg, and no infection or lameness would ensue.

Don limped back to the house with me dragging behind nursing my hand. His pants were torn in several places, and bruises were starting to form in the openings. "If we only could have convinced him it was for his own good," he mumbled, "would have made it a lot easier." I nodded in agreement and suggested that we needed some corral facilities in case there was a next time.

A week later I saw Don at the lumberyard, buying supplies for a new barn and pens. "I started thinking about what you said the other day, about there being a next time," he explained. "I realized you might be a little harder to get a hold of if we had another veterinary emergency with Jefferson. So I'm starting the project this weekend." He hesitated, then spoke again. "Besides, my wife spotted another porcupine in the pasture this morning."

Who's the Boss?

Although most veterinary clinics have an owner or at least an office manager, the real boss doesn't have a name on the sign out front, a big office or a lot of framed certificates on the wall But the real boss does get a private litter box.

Just about every practice has a mascot cat, and these lucky animals always act as if they are running the show. The feline in charge will often strut, tail straight in the air, through the exam room to check out the quality of patient care or leap onto the operating table to ruin the sterile surgery area. If the waiting room is filled with lowly canines, the cat may peruse the area, testing the strength of owners and their leashes. If bored with harassing the patrons, the feline will assume a supervisory position on the reception counter. This allows the animal to take on a public relations role as well by generously giving human clients the opportunity to caress it while paying their bills.

The application for Clinic Cat is not a simple one. Most find their way into this position because they were strays that no one wanted or hard luck cases that needed expensive medical treatment, and no one returned to pick them up. No matter how they end up at the office, they will eventually win the hearts of the humans and climb the corporate ladder quickly.

My favorite Boss Cat was a beautiful gray tabby appropriately named Beastie Cat. She was found on the crest of a nearby mountain pass scrounging out an existence for herself and seven kittens. They were probably dumped off by someone who was disappointed when one feline pet became eight. This above-timberline environment was no place to be raising a family; small rodent meals are scarce and so is shelter, not to mention an abundance of wind, cold and lightning storms. But Beastie Cat must have been quite a mountaineer and an innovative hunter because she and her family fared pretty well.

My boss was out on a Jeep ride when he stumbled upon the feline family, and they were more than willing to jump in with him. On their arrival at the clinic they were treated as if they had checked into the Spa at the Ritz. Everybody was bathed, brushed and dewormed. Next they were treated to a daily buffet of gourmet cat food, and within two weeks all signs of a tough lifestyle had fallen away. They were given full run of the clinic, which became a rumpus room for the kittens. Sliding across the linoleum floors and holding "fur ball" wrestling meets provided hours of entertainment for all of us. Christie didn't enjoy their antics as much as the rest of us since she got the job of maintaining the litter box, a task that got bigger by the day. As she said with a scoop in one hand, "All they do is eat and . . !" Beastie Cat was not that amused with her kittens' rambunctious behavior either. She spent exhausting days attempting to keep some kind of order within her brood, a losing proposition for even the best of feline families.

The day came when it was time to find the kittens new homes. They easily found cozy *casas* with great clients, but Mom was not so lucky although it's true she had a few traits that made her a less-than-perfect house pet. Physically she was fine; her problems were definitely more psychological. We would often find her lying on her back in the middle of the clinic driveway, feet straight up in the air. By some miracle she never got run over. Sometimes she got along with the other animals that came through the door. and sometimes she didn't. If she didn't care for a patient she would welcome the animal in the door by hissing and spitting as if to say, "How dare you disturb me, even if you do have a life-threatening injury?" Occasionally a curious dog would get too close and get a razor-sharp claw across the snout. Owners never seemed to see the humor in their puppy leaving the office with a nose full of sutures when he was only there for a rabies vaccination. We never ruled out the possibility that she was demonically possessed, nor was an exorcism considered out of the question. She was a little bit of a liability, but she was always entertaining, and besides, no one else would have her. Some days her mental illness actually seemed to be cured. She would be friendly, personable and affectionate. Then, the next day her attitude might be closer to that of a mountain lion with a migraine.

Beastie not only targeted clients and patients; the staff was not immune to her bad-hair days either. It was not uncommon for her to bite one of us for no reason at all or lash out at our hands with her paw while we were writing out a prescription. At one point she developed an ear infection and was less than happy about having her ear canal irrigated. The next morning I didn't notice the thank-you gift she had left for me on my chair until it was too late. An unfamiliar feeling against my jeans and then the very familiar odor of cat feces let me know she had reaped her vengeance. How do you get back at a cat for that?

My most memorable Beastie Cat experience occurred on a lazy July Sunday afternoon. I was on the couch in the middle of one of those coming-of-age TV movies that I had seen at least five times before. I still had the same television that my roommate and I bought out of the paper in college for $12—one of those with a lot of wood and large cloth-covered speakers on each side. The movie was just about to put me to sleep when my pager threw a curve in my afternoon. I returned the call to find that there would be no nap today.

"Our German shepherd jumped off the deck to chase a squire, and now he won't put any weight on his front left leg. Can you take a look at him?" Mr. Miller asked. I could tell from his voice that he had been hoping my boss would be the one to call him back, but I would have to do on short notice. They would meet me at the clinic in five minutes, and I was dreading it. I pulled into the driveway and was hit by that familiar smell of pine produced by the old-growth ponderosa that surrounded the parameter of the building. The 40-foot giants seemed to take away some of the stress and sterility from the veterinary hospital atmosphere.

The Millers were nice enough, but their kids were out of control. Mr. Miller was a quiet, hardworking man of about 45 with graying hair and a perpetually exhausted appearance. Mrs. Miller was very similar in female form, except she appeared even more worn out than her mate. Their five children—all loud, spoiled and completely devoid of manners—were making their lives a living hell.. The kids ranged in age from about four to 15, and the entire brood was running around the building rattling door knobs when I got to the clinic.

Mrs. Miller finally yelled out from their old Subaru wagon, "Come on, kids, if you're not good we won't let you watch if there's any blood involved." Even though it sounded like a good argument, especially for this crew of miscreants, the "Brady Bunch" continued to attempt their break-in. I wanted to pull back out the driveway and hotfoot it back to my cabin, but I had to get it together for the dog's sake. After managing to unlock the door amid the chaos, I stood back as the entire family flooded into the waiting room. Mr. Miller and I carried the big dog into the exam room and eased him onto the Formica exam table.

My examination of the leg elicited a yelp when I flexed the carpal joint above the paw. I informed the spectators that we needed to take an x-ray, and they all nodded their approval. Even the four-year-old gave me the OK. Mr. Miller helped me get Scout into the radiology area and then went back out with the rest of the pack to avoid radiation exposure. After strapping on the fashionable lead apron and matching gloves, I talked Scout into allowing me to snap a couple of different views. This was all taking some time, and I could sense the natives getting a little restless in the next room. By the time the films were soaked in developing chemicals, the children were bouncing around the clinic as if it were one of those inflatable castles that people rent for birthday parties. They had opened every door,

helped themselves to the bandage materials and removed my diploma from the wall to determine whether or not I was qualified to be treating their pet. The parents had obviously given up on discipline and looked like they were longing for the days of life without offspring. The Millers were elated to hear that Scout had no fractures and could go home with just a support wrap. They were also very relieved to avoid the expense of surgery.

Meanwhile, the reform school candidates had moved back into the waiting room, and the noise level was reaching an all-time high. But despite the racket, I could suddenly hear a low, deep growl from behind the counter. Beastie Cat had been napping on the receptionist's chair the entire time, and now she was awakened. As I strode down the short hallway, I felt like I was in slow motion trying to reach the waiting room before the inevitable happened, but it was too late. There was a serpent-like hiss followed by a scream and a stampede of footsteps out the door. All that remained from the incident by the time I arrived was a triumphant feline whipping her tail as if to tempt a rematch and a few drops of human blood on the floor. Mrs. Miller, the only family member still in the building, stood back from the counter holding her open checkbook.

It took all my strength to hold back laughter as I wrote up the bill, fully expecting a comment about our ill-mannered kitty, but it didn't happen. Mrs. Miller thanked me profusely "We really appreciate you taking care of old Scout," she said. "We weren't sure about you at first, but now we feel comfortable with you if no one else is available." I didn't allow myself to think of an appropriate response to that. As they drove away I could see the children all sitting quietly in the old car. Beastie had accomplished what the parents could not.

Two weeks later they brought Scout back in for a recheck. The family filed in one by one and sat silently in the plastic chairs. Beastie Cat lay on the counter staring them down while slapping her tail rhythmically against the surface, but no one challenged her. I appreciated that cat a lot more from then on. In fact, I even learned to overlook most of her psychotic episodes.

Slap Shot

One of my favorite places to make a house call is a guest ranch tucked into the Rockies beside a beautiful mountain river. The ranch consists of a main lodge with outlying stone and log buildings with views of snowy peaks. They keep 70 horses of every color, age and breed. People come from all around the world to stay at the ranch and trail ride for a week at a time With this many animals, the ranch keeps me busy, especially during the summer months. On one particular day they needed some routine maintenance done on some horses who were getting the week off. So Christie brushed the crumbs from my previous day's lunch off the passenger seat of the pickup, shook her head at me and crawled in for our ride to the guest ranch.

As I steered the truck out the driveway and onto the risky mountain highway, Christie started organizing the paperwork on my dash. I always had a mess of receipts on my dash, but it never seemed to bother her before. She was abnormally quiet that morning, and I had a feeling I knew what the problem might be related to. Christie had met a guy about a month before and was very excited about this one. I had met him briefly at the clinic—too brief an encounter to make a proper judgment, I admit, but I've never trusted men with excessive jewelry.

After 10 minutes of Christie's paper shuffling, my urge to plunge into dangerous territory overwhelmed me. "So . . . how was your weekend?" I tried. No response; we sat in uncomfortable silence for the next couple of minutes.

Finally, she spoke, eyes still focused out the window. "Men suck!"

Oh boy, I thought, now I'd opened the can. "OK, what happened?"

She stared down at her lap. "I mentioned that my parents wanted to have us over for supper," she began, "and he gave me the 'maybe we should date other people' talk. Then he moved onto his 'I'm not looking for a long-term relationship' finale."

I wondered what I should say. I wasn't surprised that this happened. Most guys consider those lines to be standard fare, not that I would know recently since I hadn't had a date in months. The best I could come up with was, "Well, maybe it's for the best." This just got me an icy glare and more silence, but she needed to talk to someone about it, so that didn't last too long. She went on about how she had thought this might be "the guy" and how much they had in common. Having heard this all before from her about other guys, I decided it would be safest just to nod my head and throw in an occasional "uh huh." At last we pulled off the highway and down the windy gravel road into the guest ranch.

Four horses were tied to the hitching rail just outside the barn where the saddles and tack were kept. At the sound of our truck an overdressed 20-something wrangler strode out of the barn. He had on the classic black felt cowboy hat and tight jeans. His shirt had ivory buttons and a yoke design on the front and back. But the clothes were pressed and new, not well-used like those of someone who was working hard. He was obviously very proud of his outfit and shoved out his chest when he saw Christie get out of the truck.

He stuck out his hand to me. "I'm Shane from Fort Worth. Got lots of experience with horses. Back home we wouldn't have hired a vet to do this; we'd have done it ourselves." I was starting to see why Shane had been left behind to "help us" instead of taking out rides with the others.

The first three horses had sharp points on their back teeth that needed to be filed off so they could chew better. This procedure is known as teeth floating. As we worked down the row, I was amused by Shane's attempts to flirt with Christie. Of course she completely ignored his overtures to the point that I was actually getting a little embarrassed for him. The last equine was having some trouble urinating and needed to have his sheath cleaned. I gave him some sedation to make the procedure safer and easier, then waited patiently for it to take effect, trying at the same time to distract Shane from Christie by making small talk about Texas.

After a few minutes the sedation started to kick in, and the horse's head began to drop. The other side effect of the sedative is that the part that needed to be cleaned dropped down also. This situation is usually accompanied by a few marginal jokes and snickers, but that day the audience reaction could not have had worse timing. Shane cleared his throat. All I could think was, "Oh, no, please don't," but here it came anyway. He leaned against the horse with one arm, crossed his legs and said, "Well, you know, this horse doesn't have anything on me" in his best Texas drawl.

I turned immediately towards Christie. Her face was beet red, not with embarrassment, but anger. She was completely fed up with men, and this poor excuse for one had put her over the edge. Her blue eyes narrowed into demonic slits, and her face contorted into a shape I hadn't seen before. She cut loose on him with expletives not to be repeated and sent him off with his tail between his legs. I debated about calling the liability insurance company right then or waiting to see how things panned out. We finished our work in silence and without Shane.

On our way back to the clinic Christie's tough exterior started to melt away, and as she softened the tears began to come. "I'm sorry, I never should have reacted that way, but that guy was being such a jerk," she squeaked out between the tears.

Searching for the right words, the best I could come up with was, " Well, you've just got a lot going on today, don't you think?" She nodded and we continued down the highway, laughing about Shane's obvious insecurities intermingled with a complete lack of taste.

It was only about a week after the "men suck" incident when I had to return to the ranch for an evening emergency. That night an animal dealt out the punishment to an unsuspecting Shane that Christie would have liked to give him.

This particular summer evening I was called to the ranch to treat a horse with a bellyache. A sweet young woman from Georgia came out to the corral to help me. She filled me in on the animal's symptoms, and we agreed that colic was the problem. Colic in horses is usually caused by some form of blockage in the intestine and makes them extremely uncomfortable since they cannot vomit. This poor horse was no exception, and we both just wanted to make him feel better. I placed a plastic tube through the patient's nose and down to the stomach, then pumped mineral oil through the tube to help get his bowels moving. After that I gave him an injection of painkiller, and within a few minutes the horse started looking for something to eat.

I was packing to leave when a couple of the male employees came out of the lodge moving in the direction of the burro pen. The two burros were named Lefty and Poncho. They were a mangy pair with long shaggy hair that hung over their eyes and broom-like tails that would whip back and forth when they were upset. Burros are not large animals but are extremely strong for their size. They have a low center of gravity and are very hard to hang onto if they decide they'd rather not be. These two were especially tough since they had been wild originally and brought in from the desert a few years before as part of a rescue effort.

As the two young men moved across in front of us in the last of the day's sunlight, I recognized one of them as Shane. His confidence had been built back up by the beers he had with dinner, and he had decided to attempt to ride Lefty. This was entertainment I could not resist getting a good seat for since Lefty had never been ridden. One

might be tempted to worry about Lefty's well-being, but this would only be a worry if you hadn't been around burros.

The slightly tipsy wanna-be cowboy hauled himself over the corral fence, grabbed a halter and headed for Lefty. He got the halter on the burro's head and attached a lead rope to it. Then, with a boost from his cohort he was on Lefty's back. He let out a "yee ha!" and then the games began. The second Shane's butt and Lefty's back made contact, Lefty leaped straight up, all four feet off the ground as if he were jet propelled. I could see at least three feet of light between rider and beast before they slammed to earth for the second round. Lefty had barely touched down before he kicked both back legs into the air and shot his rider towards the stars. Shane might have been willing to call it quits at that point except for the fact that Lefty wasn't done with him yet. As only a burro could, Lefty regrouped and kicked him in the groin on his way back to earth.

In a matter of seconds the burro had completely debilitated his human challenger and was back to munching on hay as if nothing had happened. The young wrangler lay moaning in a pile of donkey manure as I headed toward my pickup. I understand he didn't boast about anything the rest of the summer.

The next time I saw Shane was about a week later, and he still wasn't walking right. He moved as if he were trying to hold a bowling ball between his legs. The rest of the staff said he hadn't been even close to getting back on a horse since his dance with Lefty. I can't imagine what hours in a saddle would have felt like to a man in his condition.

Christie seemed to think his predicament was quite humorous. She did deserve her revenge, but as a fellow Y chromosome holder, I couldn't help feeling a little sorry for him. I guess you could call it "sympathy pain."

Attention Deficit

As on so many nights since graduation from veterinary school, I heard the sound that makes me immediately sit straight up in bed. Sometimes it seems that this noise is part of a dream—a fire alarm or a school bell telling me I'm late for class. After shaking off the dream that night, I was hit by the harsh reality that it was my pager, so I would probably have to get out of bed and take off into the night. At the least I would have to wake myself up enough to call these people back and act completely prepared to deal with whatever four-legged emergency they had.

Just as so many nights before I picked up the phone beside my bed and dialed the number that showed on my pager. After about eight rings a sleepy male voice on the other end answered. Explaining that I was Dr. Wells returning his call about the sick dog, I was met by a brief silence followed by some expletives about how late it was and the slamming down of the phone. Now I was really awake.

Dialing the correct number this time, I reached Mrs. Feller, who explained that her new shih tzu puppy, Hercules, was practically unconscious and needed to be seen right away. Her voice was shaky, nearly breaking down into a full-blown cry. I told her to head for the clinic and I would meet her there. Pulling on my clothes, I went out into the night to warm up my truck and drove, blurry eyed, to the clinic—a route so familiar that the vehicle seemed to maneuver the route on its own.

By the time I reached the clinic Mrs. Feller was already sitting in the parking lot. She was a well-dressed, soccer mom-type accessorized with the appropriate battleship SUV. Standing on the clinic's wooden deck with her, I rifled through my keys trying three different ones before finding the one that worked. Mrs. Feller watched me anxiously, waiting to get her ailing puppy inside for treatment. Finally getting the door opened, I fumbled in the dark for the light switch to bring the clinic to life.

At last we were in the exam room, and Mrs. Feller lay the small and nearly comatose pup on the exam table. The poor little guy was nothing but fur-covered bones as he lay there on the cold Formica tabletop, his chest rising slowly with every labored breath. I stared down at him with a sickening feeling in my stomach. I had no idea what to do next—not an uncommon response for a young veterinarian to have. There was no sign of trauma or fever to indicate an infection. His heart and lungs also sounded normal. Sweat was beginning to run down my nose.

Mrs. Feller began to pick up on my lack of a diagnosis. "Do you have any idea what is wrong with him?" she asked, obviously getting a little nervous about my abilities. I ignored her doubt for the moment and began asking her all the appropriate questions: Was there something Hercules could have eaten from the garbage? Would anyone have had reason to poison him? As I continued to try to pry something helpful from the puppy's history, I noticed Mrs. Feller start to fidget a little. She wouldn't look at me, staring only at the lifeless little dog. It seemed like she had something to say but couldn't quite get it out.

Eventually I stopped asking questions, giving her the opportunity to speak. After about a minute she spoke up. "I took Hercules to another veterinary clinic earlier in the week for a diarrhea problem. They prescribed some medicine for an intestinal parasite, so I picked it up at a local pharmacy that afternoon." She didn't want to tell me this because she was afraid I wouldn't see her dog if I had known that we were not her regular veterinarians. Of course, the other clinic did not see after-hours emergencies.

After fessing up she began to tell me about how they had moved from California the previous year with their first shih tzu, Spike. Not long after arriving in the Rocky Mountains they let Spike out to do his routine business. But that particular November evening the first snow of the season was falling hard. Unfortunately, neither Spike nor his family was very familiar with mountain snowstorms, and Spike never returned to the house. Tears filled Mrs. Feller's eyes as she explained how they found Spike the following spring. He had been near a favorite spot next to the curb when the snow plow had come by. I realized that this had been quite a stress on the family, and now the dog they had gotten to replace him was deteriorating right in front of me.

"Is there anything else you can think of that might have triggered his illness?" I asked hopefully.

She gave it one more try. "Well, you know, he didn't really start going downhill until I started the intestinal treatment." She dumped her purse out onto the table, and an amber pill bottle rolled free of the other contents.

A close study of the bottle showed these to be the appropriate tablets, but the dosage seemed a little high. I excused myself and headed for the back of the clinic to check the drug formulary. I didn't want her to realize that I didn't know the exact dose of every possible pharmaceutical for every size of dog. To my astonishment, Hercules had been getting the correct dose—for an adult Saint Bernard. Not having much experience with this kind of overdose, I decided it would be best to contact Poison Control.

The expert on call yawned as she looked up the treatment for this specific toxicity. "How much did you say that the pup was getting?"

When I gave her the numbers I heard a little gasp on the other end of the line. "I have never heard of an overdose that large for this medication," she said, sounding very much awake.

After these words of encouragement, I followed her instructions for treatment. I.V. fluids seemed to be the main component of the protocol, so I dug out the smallest catheter that I could find and shaved Hercules' left front leg to accentuate the cephalic vein. No magic cure or foolproof antidote was available, just fluids to accelerate the drug's elimination through the puppy's kidneys. Getting an I.V. catheter into his tiny vein was like threading a python through the eye of a needle. In addition to the blood vessel being small to begin with, the pup was severely dehydrated, which further decreased the diameter of the vein. After poking and prodding for several very tense minutes, with Mrs. Feller glaring over my shoulder, I gave up on getting the catheter placed in that vein. At this point I thought I heard her mumble something about how long I had been out of school. Fortunately, dogs have two front legs, and luck was with me on the right one. With everything ready to go, I hooked up a bag of fluids and put Hercules on a heated pad in one of the stainless steal kennels. Now it was out of our hands; I just hoped it wasn't too late.

I discussed the less-than-favorable prognosis with Mrs. Feller, and she went home for what remained of the night, leaving me alone with the little patient. The fluid dripped in very slowly; if it is run in too quickly a dog's lungs will fill with fluid, so patience is a virtue. Pulling up the most comfortable office chair we had, I began to settle in Sleep started to become harder to fight quickly, and I drifted in and out, occasionally waking up just enough to check on Hercules' condition.

I had no idea how much time had passed when the shrill yipping of a very upset little dog woke me suddenly Rubbing the sleep out of my eyes, I could see the sun peeking through the small window beside the kennels in the back room of the clinic where Hercules and I had spent the night. The plastic clock on the wall said six a.m. It took me a moment to realize that the persistent barking was coming from Hercules.

He was bouncing around in the cage, tangled up in the I.V. tubing and looking for food. His little eyes were bright, and his pink tongue was wagging in happiness. I got up out of my chair and found myself standing in a pool of dog urine. It was all that was left of the overdose. This was one of the few times I was happy about standing in such a puddle. As I filled Hercules' dog dish he nearly took off my finger to get to the food Mrs. Feller was elated when I called her with the good news and couldn't get off the phone fast enough to come pick him up.

It is easy to make this kind of a call, especially when there was a good chance things could have gone the other way. Making the phone calls to convey the opposite outcome is one of my least favorite responsibilities of veterinary practice. Curing an animal that is so ill gives one a great deal of satisfaction. I especially look forward to seeing such patients again for routine visits to follow their progress after these kinds of serious ordeals, but I never saw Hercules again. Mrs. Feller explained to Christie that she would rather see an older, more experienced practitioner, and she returned to her previous veterinarian for Hercules' future care.

Intestinal Fortitude

I am often asked if animal injuries gross me out or make me sick. Many people tell me they could not handle the blood and don't know how I can deal with it on a regular basis. I'm sure most veterinarians don't think about wounds and injuries in that way. Caring for the animal is a given, but making it better as quickly as possible is our responsibility. We are trained to immediately evaluate patients medically, coming up with a plan to put them back together. This training helps us focus in a way that keeps us from freaking out.

I remember dreading the first day of anatomy lab in veterinary school, wondering if I could handle it and being afraid of vomiting in front of my fellow students. I hung tough, but not all of my classmates were as fortunate. As with many things in life, the first day was hard, but every day that followed got a little easier. We knew we had to get through these classes to be able to better care for sick and injured animals in practice. The problem is that as practicing veterinarians, we sometimes forget our clients have not had the same experiences and may not always react well to their own pets' injuries.

As a new graduate I was often so involved in repairing a wound that I would forget about what the owner was going through. Sometimes I would get so excited about a particular type of case that had not crossed my exam table before but had been discussed at length in a sleepy, post-lunch lecture a couple of years earlier that I would be oblivious to the owners' concern for their pet. I'm sure my excitement made matters worse for a few of my early clients.

As time progressed I began to gain enough confidence to work on a pet while explaining the procedure and prognosis to the owners at the same time. Still, it became apparent that some owners were not handling the sight of the wounds well, even getting a little woozy despite my clinical explanations. For some reason, debriding and suturing lacerations seemed to bother people as much as anything, and on one Colorado summer day I was about to experience just how much.

I had been in the clinic most of the morning, neutering a couple of young cats the Humane Society had dropped off. They were not actually happy to be there, and it required a lot of patience to even coax them out of the live animal traps in which they had been caught. These traps were the favorite feline transport device of the Humane Society since many cats they brought in had very little human exposure. The cats were typically neglected or driven to the mountains and dropped off to fend for themselves. One could not blame them for their lack of trust, yet they still needed to be vaccinated and neutered.

The society volunteers would place a morsel of tuna in one end of the cage, and when the hungry kitty wandered in they tripped the release, causing the door to close behind the cat. While the caretakers had the best intentions, they were not willing to actually remove the cats from the traps—this honor was saved for the vet.

Since both my employer and I had nearly been disfigured during this process before, we had devised a much safer removal method. We would place a large plastic bag around the entire apparatus, connecting the open end to the gas anesthesia machine. After a few minutes the feline would be sleeping soundly, keeping its stress and ours to a minimum. Although this proved to be a great way to handle feral cats, it was a time-consuming way to prepare an animal for surgery, and I was ready for some Rocky Mountain sunshine by the time I headed out to see an injured horse.

The animal belonged to Joe Taylor, a retired marine who now flew a Flight for Life chopper for a hospital in town. I always envied Joe a little because he was still in great shape at 55. He had maintained a regulation crew cut peppered with gray and treated his horse, Sarge, like he was army issue. The big bay Morgan had no wants. Joe spent at least one hour a day grooming him, and the lucky horse always received five-star hay. Joe was very proud of Sarge, and he was horrified to find him with a four-inch cut on the end of his nose that morning. The horse had found an exposed nail on the barn wall that Joe was sure to eliminate the minute I had repaired the injury.

The drive to the Taylor place was beyond picturesque. The road followed a small stream through a grassy valley that was guarded at the far end by a massive, 13,000-foot peak. The scene always made me feel insignificant, knowing it had looked this way for thousands of years and would remain the same for thousands more. (That is, if it can escape the scourge of development that ravages the Rocky Mountains—but that's another story.)

On arrival I pulled up to the neatly kept little barn and met Joe in the doorway. You could tell by his expression that he wished I could have gotten there earlier but was too nice a guy to say anything. "Good to see you, Doc," he said. Then, after the most minimal pause he thought he could get away with, he added, "Sarge doesn't look too good; he's right this way." He led me into the barn where the big horse stood in cross ties. The four-inch cut ran from his right nostril to just above his lip on the left side. The edges were very smooth, as if the wound had been opened with a scalpel blade or, in Sarge's case, the point of a 16-penny nail.

Even though the blood had long dried around the edges, I knew the scarring would be minimal. The face has such a concentrated blood supply that it heals beautifully and more quickly than other part of the body, making the one who sews up a facial wound look like a hero.

After looking at the wound I headed towards the truck to gather the needed supplies. "You won't need any painkillers or sedation for old Sarge—he's a tough one," Joe called after me. For a minute I imagined the horse gritting his teeth as I forced the suture needle through the sensitive skin of his soft nose. Then I suggested that it would be easier for me if we used some sedation and local anesthetic. There was no way I would ever put an animal through unnecessary pain or anxiety when we have plenty of safe medications to prevent it.

I drew up a syringe full of tranquilizer and injected it into the Morgan's left jugular vein. As I returned to the truck for some lidocaine and instruments, Sarge started to get sleepy. His head dropped below his withers as he concentrated to keep his balance. Joe held his head steady, allowing me to inject the local just under the skin along the edges of the wound. The tissue bubbled up where the numbing fluid was forced in, desensitizing the area I would be reconstructing. The whole time Joe reassured the drunken horse that everything would be fine and that the scar would give him character. I think that I even caught Joe kissing Sarge's fuzzy brown ear when I was not supposed to be looking.

Next, I cleaned the wound aggressively with Betadine soap and positioned myself to repair it. The last stage before suturing is to increase the probability of the skin healing together by removing a tiny strip of tissue from the exposed edges. This procedure allows fresh blood to flow back into the wound, and I could have sworn Joe choked a little during this procedure. Clamping the needle in the appropriate instrument, I began the familiar interrupted suture pattern that would return the animal's nose to normal. By this time I could feel Joe's warm breath on my neck. He had repositioned himself behind me and was looking over my shoulder in a sort of supervisory position. He spoke about how many times he had seen people with wounds 10 times as severe and chuckled about past colleagues who could not handle the gruesome sight.

I was not able to concentrate both on his conversation and the face lift at the same time, so my brain automatically shut Joe off. After

about 10 minutes of sewing, I was carefully placing the last suture and explaining the after-care instructions to Joe. The nose looked a little Frankenstein-like with the ligatures in it, but Sarge would be as good as new once they were removed. "Well Joe," I said while observing my handiwork, "do you want to remove the sutures yourself, or do you want me to come back in a couple weeks and do it?" There was no response from behind me. I started to wonder if he thought my work was sub-par or if he was just in awe.

I tried again, rubbing Sarge gently on the forehead to soothe him as I spoke. "So, Joe, what do you think?" Still no answer. I was beginning to think he was being just downright rude. Even if he was dissatisfied, he could at least come up with some type of polite answer. Straightening up slowly, I turned to face my client, but he wasn't there. Instead of admiring my work, he was flat on his back in the middle of the barn floor. He had passed out cold halfway through the repair, and I hadn't even noticed. After elevating his head and feet, I watched the color flow back into his face, and he slowly started to stir. Eventually, he regained consciousness and immediately began to apologize in embarrassment. Even though Joe had experienced the sight of many grotesque human injuries during his life, the blood of an animal he so adored finished him.

Since that day, I have had many clients pass out on me. I have lost them at their barns and in the clinic. Sometimes I've been able to catch them across the exam table before they met the floor, but more than once an owner's head has dented the drywall during a procedure to treat a loved pet. After the first few times I got better at recognizing the warning signs, including the lack of conversation, pale face and glazed-over eyes. But I've learned that probably the best clue to a potential fainter is when the person brags about not being queasy.

Biker Dog

The Rocky Mountain region is full of fascinating people from all walks of life, and one day I found myself face-to-face with one of the more interesting. Mama, as she was known around town, was clutching her beloved dog while I cleaned up the "road rash" on his left hip.

The first time I had observed Mama, I was eating dinner with some friends at a local Italian restaurant. We were in the middle of some form of pasta and marinara when I noticed the noise level in the room was on the increase in order to compete with the incessant barking coming from the parking lot. It was a crystal clear mountain evening, so all the windows and doors were wide open for the comfort of the patrons. Unfortunately, this allowed the ear-piercing yipping to flow through the restaurant unchallenged. About the time that I thought the conversation could not get any louder, a stout woman at the bar with a black Harley leather jacket, a long gray braid and arms completely concealed by tattoos turned from her beer to the row of motorcycles parked out front. She proceeded to scream at the top of her lungs, "Megadeth! Megadeth! Shut yer pie hole!" This announcement quieted the entire restaurant—but not the barking dog outside. It took a few more reprimands for Megadeth to back down and the restaurant to return to a more natural conversation level.

I was dying to get a peek at the demon outside, so I faked a trip to the restroom in order to peer out into the parking lot. I was more than surprised to see that the only canine on the premises was a tiny Chihuahua seated squarely on the seat of a motorcycle, staring longingly into the bar. He was sporting a black leather vest edged with rhinestones that had a skull and crossbones on the back. The attire and motorcycle seemed to give the small dog the confidence of a German shepherd, yet he looked more like some kind of post-nuke mutant.

His eyes bulged from their sockets, and his larger-than-life, paper-thin ears added to his alien appearance. Mama had squelched his confidence for the moment, so he eventually crawled into one of the saddlebags that hung off each side of the Harley behind the seat. In fact, I learned later, this is the position that Megadeth was most commonly seen in. He would sit in the saddlebag, his head sticking out the top just enough for his ears to catch the breeze. His eyes were protected by a pair of black "doggles" that matched the goggles that Mama wore.

The two were a common sight in our mountain area, cruising together up and down the winding roads. But on this day they were in the clinic, and the road trips were going to have to be postponed for a while.

Mama explained that Megadeth had been nestled in his usual position when she swerved to miss a large rock that had fallen onto the pavement as they often do when the ice melts in the spring. She had been able to avoid the rock, but Megadeth was ejected from his leather sidecar onto the concrete, where he slid on his side for about 10 feet. The fall and subsequent slide sheered off the hair and some skin from the little dog's side.

Mama had flown up our driveway like Evel Knievel and burst into the clinic with the little dog cradled in her muscular arms. He was wrapped in her black leather jacket, soaked through with Chihuahua blood. She gently laid him on the exam table and her tears began to flow. This wasn't unusual, of course. Often when people get their injured pet to the veterinarian, they feel that they have completed their task of being in charge and can turn over the reins of control to the veterinarian. Then the true emotions come through. The tough lady was now looking at me more like a frightened child than a seasoned biker.

After giving the little guy a thorough exam, I realized that the only serious injury he had sustained was a potato chip-sized open sore over the hip. The skin from this section had been left behind on the pavement, and what remained looked like raw meat sprinkled with tiny pebbles ground in from the slide. I explained to Mama that he was going to be fine, but the wound would require a lot of care over the next month. Since there was really nothing left to suture, it would have to remain open and heal in from the edges. Mama agreed to care for Megadeth's injuries diligently, so we got started right away.

Hands that could bend steel gently held the trembling pup while I picked the rock out of the dried blood that coated the lesion. Like most owners, she was a little nervous about holding her injured pet while treatment was being performed. As Megadeth struggled to avoid my cleansing, Mama's grip tightened around his neck. I asked her to ease off a couple of times, but as soon as he flinched her adrenaline kicked in, and the strong hands contracted back to full force. Unfortunately, too much restraint around the neck of a small dog breed with bulging eyes, such as shih tzus, Boston terriers and this Chihuahua, can dramatically increase the pressure in the animal's head. Megadeth's patience had just about run out, so he made a final attempt to turn his head and bite my hand. Mama panicked even more, her grip tightened further and the dog's right eye popped completely out of its socket! It hung there, dangling only by the tiny eye muscles and optic nerve. Hollywood special-effects people could not have produced a more horrifying scene.

When Mama saw the expelled eyeball, she began to gag and ran from the room in tears. I yelled for Christie and she came running in to help. We quickly anesthetized the little canine and after a couple minutes of manipulation had the elusive eyeball back in its socket. I had been through this many times with small exophthalmic dogs that ended up on the losing end of a canine dispute and were brought in with displaced peepers, but never had I seen it happen right in front of me.

In order to keep the eyeball in place, the lids had to be sutured closed until the inflammation receded, allowing the eye to achieve its original fit. Taking advantage of the anesthetic we also finished cleaning the wound on the dog's hip.

I went out to the waiting room to talk with Mama while Christie waited for the patient to wake up. After explaining to Mama that her beloved pet would be fine and probably retain most of the sight in the newly reset eye, her fear turned to guilt. She felt terrible about her excessive use of force but seemed to feel better when I exaggerated just a little about how commonly this exact situation occurred.

We loaded her up with anti-inflammatories and antibiotics and sent the pair on their way. This time the motorcycle pulled out of the driveway at a much slower pace.

I wondered several times over the next week how Mama and Megadeth were getting along. The answer came to me as I was driving down the highway to check on a lame horse when a woman on a motorcycle passed me on a double yellow. Yes, it was Mama with Megadeth in his usual spot. He sat in his tough-guy stance, except a couple of new accessories had been added. On top of his head was a helmet fashioned out of half a black, plastic ball. An old shoestring wrapped under his jaw held it on, and over his right eye was a tiny leather patch that would have made even the fiercest of pirates proud. Even after the eye was completely healed and sutures removed, I would occasionally spot him sporting the patch like a badge of honor. Mama said it made him feel more like a "real tough biker dog." Eventually, she forgot which eye she had made the patch for. Thus, in the months that followed he could be seen with it over either eye, but the effect was the same—for Megadeth *and* for onlookers.

A Hog
in the House

Pets obviously come in every size, shape and color. They can be mammalian, reptilian or avian Pigs are probably one of the more unusual pets, especially when they live in the house. Being from rural Iowa—that is, hog country—I have to admit that I found it a little strange when Korean potbellied pigs became so popular as house pets. The fad seemed to sweep the country, and these funny animals became quite an expensive commodity. It became almost a status symbol to own one. They are relatively small hogs as long as they are not overfed. But since restricting feed is nearly impossible for most pet lovers, including me, the result can be 200-plus-pound porcine pals sharing the couch. They are meant to live on a diet of fruits and vegetables, yet I have observed these spoiled potbellies ingesting everything from marshmallows to cornflakes.

Their skin is dark and almost scaly with sparse long hairs pro-truding like porcupine quills. Not big on looks, the name "potbellied" is well deserved. Their pendulous abdomen hangs so low to the ground it often drags on the floor as they wander about the house.

Loading these misshapen porcine companions in the car can be a little tough, so we usually have to see them on their own turf. Most commonly they are sprawled out on the kitchen floor with a cushy dog bed between their tough hide and the linoleum. Mrs. Chandler's pig, Bacon, was no exception. He lay snoring in his place of honor near the heat vent when I arrived in response to his owner's call. Mrs. Chandler had to step over him to get to the refrigerator, stove and counter where the children sat eating breakfast. She moved about the room gracefully, stepping over the pig without missing a beat as if he were one of the kitchen furnishings since this was where he spent most of his time and the Chandlers had accepted it. I had witnessed this routine several times before due to the fact that Bacon required a hoof trim and vaccinations once a year.

The Chandlers had a beautiful modern kitchen with dark granite countertops and stainless steel appliances, but a couple of features were clearly not standard Home Depot issue: the refrigerator and oven had large metal latches screwed onto the doors. When my curiosity got the best of me on a previous visit and I asked about these, the family informed me that Bacon was capable of opening the doors and stealing the contents before these burglar-proof latches were installed.

I arrived that day to take care of Bacon's annual treatment. Some might think this would be a fairly easy task, but these would be people who had very little experience with pigs. Bacon had to be anesthetized for his pedicure. He hated the injection and screamed at the top of his lungs in anticipation. The same scene played out every time. Bacon ran around the kitchen squealing and skating on the slick floor as I chased after him, clutching the syringe like a knife. I had tried sneaking up on him, even crawling across the floor on my hands and knees, but he always spotted me at the last minute. Finally I would corner him long enough to inject the drugs, and Bacon would drift off, at last ending the ear-piercing part of the ordeal. By the time the excessive hoof was cut off and the appropriate vaccinations given, he would already have begun to come around, and he would be fully recovered in time for his next meal. This day played out no differently, and within an hour I was on my way to the next case after the usual thanks and apologies from Mrs. Chandler for my inconvenience.

About two weeks after my trip to see Bacon, Mrs. Chandler called me out again to see not only the pampered pig, but also his best friend, Buck, a yellow Labrador. The problem was that they had both escaped through the Invisible Fence and proceeded to eat an entire bag of cat food that was stored in the garage. Because the cat food was much higher in protein than they were used to, a constant stream of pungent diarrhea was coming from both animals. Much to Mrs. Chandler's disappointment, Bacon had made it back to his favorite spot in the kitchen before it hit him, turning the room into a barn lot in a matter of minutes.

If that wasn't bad enough, he dribbled through almost every room in the house before Mrs. Chandler could run him back into the yard. By this time her normally perfectly styled hair was no longer perfect, and perspiration had caused her make-up to run. She was practically crying in frustration as she mumbled something about the Invisible Fence.

When I cornered Bacon in the yard to treat him with some bismuth solution for his overactive bowels, I noticed the large collar around his thick neck, hidden under Bacon's fourth double chin. There I found the typical plastic box with two metal prongs to transfer a minimal current to the animal if it crosses the underground electric barrier. I have to admit that I'd never found one of these contraptions on a pig before. Bacon's collar had to be extended with an extra nylon strap since it was designed to fit a dog's neck. Buck also was sporting his "escape-proof" collar, which brought up the question of how both animals were able to leave the electrified backyard and get to the cat food bag in the garage.

Mrs. Chandler anticipated the bewilderment on my face and began to explain before I could even ask. "Let me show you what's going on here," she said. "Bacon is a little more than your average pet." She left Buck and Bacon in the backyard with their collars in place. Making sure that the Invisible Fence was activated, she placed

a bowl of table scraps just out of reach across the invisible barrier. Then I followed her into the house where we watched the scene unfold through a kitchen window. At first Bacon and Buck circled in the yard acting casual, trying to ignore the bait. But once Bacon decided that his owner and I were not coming back outside, he pointed his snout at the bowl with a look of determination, at which time he transformed into a wild boar ready to attack his prey in the bush. Next, his wrinkled body began to twitch and shake as if he were starting to have a seizure. A crescendo squeal came from his open mouth, and his poor excuse for a tail spun like a helicopter blade. Buck was going through a similar procedure just a couple of steps behind the pig. Then Bacon's eyes closed tightly and he lunged across the underground wire with Buck on his heals. Bacon had figured out how to psyche himself up to run past the shock of the fence, and he had taught Buck to do the same.

After the two were happily munching on their prize, Mrs. Chandler turned to me. "I guess pigs are just too darn smart for these gadgets," she said. "I just don't know how I'm going to keep him in, and now he's taught my dog how to escape also" From my rural upbringing I knew that swine could be all but impossible to contain. They use their tough, shovel-like noses to root under fences and easily exit their pens, always certain something is more interesting and potentially tasty in the world outside. In farm country, pigs are perpetually destroying gardens and ruining neighbor relations.

Over the years the Chandlers fortified their yard countless times, but Bacon always managed to escape followed by any family pet that was up for a romp. After he had ingested all the neighborhood garden contents, he would then raid the garbage cans. These little binges did not do anything for the Chandlers' popularity, but they didn't seem to be able to stop him. Finally, as Bacon began to age, he spent more time in the house and less time pillaging the countryside. Eventually he became such a sedentary old pig that the destruction completely came to an end—a relief for everyone involved, especially the Chandlers.

I hadn't heard much about Bacon for several months when we received a call one morning that Mrs. Chandler wanted me to stop by and check on him. He was lying in his old spot in the middle of the kitchen, sleeping off breakfast, when I came in. "He's not moving around much anymore, but his appetite is still good," she told me. "I pretty much give him whatever he wants these days." Beside him was a dog food bowl full of apples and chocolate chip cookies. It was hard to feel too sorry for Bacon.

I examined him only to find some arthritic joints, typical of a porcine old enough for a senior citizen discount. "He's just getting older," I explained to Mrs. Chandler and suggested she start him on some supplements for his joints. "I guess you're relieved he's not terrorizing the neighborhood anymore," I added as I patted his engorged stomach. "I'm sure he's your last pet pig?"

No response came from Mrs. Chandler. I looked up to see her rather befuddled expression. "Well, actually, we thought some young blood might keep Bacon a little more active." She walked to the back door and pushed it open just a crack. A tiny potbellied piglet tore into the room, made a couple of laps and slid to a stop in front of me. His eyes twinkled and his snout was already covered with dirt from the backyard. "Meet Pork Chop," Mrs. Chandler said. "I just couldn't resist him"

Foster Family

Everyone has heard the old adage that people tend to look like their pets, and I've found that it is often true. Most veterinarians will tell you that animals and their owners often have the same medical problems as well. Whether it is obesity or hyperthyroidism, the number of times they have the same affliction is almost uncanny. The tough part about this correlation is informing owners of their pet's situation. Often the people have been dealing with the condition themselves for years, so they know what their pet will have to go through. For obvious reasons, telling certain people that their cat is overweight, for example, can be a little uncomfortable for everyone involved and certainly disappointing for the cat. "Light" feline food often has a consistency similar to sawdust even though it is just what the overindulgent cat needs. Another hard one is telling senior citizens that their 16-year-old poodle is suffering from old age and explaining the curses of that condition. They always give me the knowing nods, indicating that they can relate, but under the surface lies the acknowledgement of their own mortality.

Thomas Gertsen had been a client for many years but had never disclosed any information about his own ailments. He was a very conscientious pet owner, sparing no expense when it came to his beloved cat Andre. Thomas was a short, heavyset man who was beginning to gray a little around the temples. He was a confirmed bachelor who spent his days fixing people's computer problems. Andre coincidentally looked very similar. He was a stocky little yellow tabby who was beginning to gray around the muzzle.

Andre usually came in only for his annual vaccinations and teeth cleaning, but one day Thomas brought him in because of some abnormal behavior. The cat had begun to drink more water and urinate more often than normal, both signs of an internal problem. After finding increased sugar in Andre's urine and blood, my suspicions were confirmed: he had diabetes and would require daily insulin injections to treat it.

A large percentage of pet owners would not be able to handle this commitment, but after an explanation of the treatment he would be required to perform, Thomas nodded and accepted the responsibility with enthusiasm. Then, he reached into his pocket and produced a glucometer along with a couple of insulin syringes. "I have been a diabetic for 20 years, so having two of us in the house won't be much of a hardship!" he declared. I had no argument with that and proceeded to show him how to give Andre the shots.

Thomas brought his pet in every month after that so we could test the blood sugar level, adjusting the insulin levels accordingly. Thomas was very diligent and Andre quite accommodating, making it relatively easy to regulate the medication. For two years the routine continued and so did Andre's stable health. But one day I received a call from Thomas saying that our patient had lost some weight and was drinking and urinating abnormally again, not really the kind of information I wanted to hear.

When he arrived in the exam room, the cat was severely dehydrated and lethargic. His beautiful yellow hair had lost its elasticity, and Andre's breath smelled a little like acetone. Unfortunately, I knew what the diagnosis would be, but I had to back it up with blood work. Thomas knew also; he had been involved in long conversations with his own physician about the potential effects of long-term diabetes. We placed a catheter in Andre's right cephalic vein and started some I.V fluids to combat his dehydration. After making Andre comfortable in a kennel, Thomas went home to wait for the lab results. Within a few hours we had them, confirming our worst fears. Andre had kidney failure—not just a mild case, but complete shutdown. The poor cat had not produced any urine in the last three hours, even after a half liter of fluids. Thomas stroked Andre's dull coat as I explained the situation. He fought back the tears, but a couple managed to escape down his pale cheeks. He nodded knowingly as I told him we needed to put his friend out of his misery.

Telling him to take all the time he needed, I left them alone together in the exam room to say their good-byes. I always feel somewhat helpless in these situations, knowing that not even the most well-chosen words can make things less painful. As veterinarians, we just do the best we can to be there for both human and animal. In about five minutes Thomas opened the door, indicating that he was as ready as he was going to be. He wanted to stay with Andre, so Christie came in to hold the cat while I injected the euthanasia solution into the catheter that we had placed earlier. Andre drifted off quietly as the rest of us stared down at him silently. Finally, Thomas eked out a "thank you," but Christie and I could only nod in acknowledgment, both knowing that if we spoke we would not be able to maintain our composure.

Euthanasia is the hardest aspect of veterinary practice yet one of the most important. Many pre-veterinary students have put an end to their career aspirations after assisting with this procedure. Some might think that it would get easier with time, but they would be so wrong.

It was hard to see Thomas leave the clinic in tears and alone. He placed the empty cat carrier into the back seat of his Honda Civic and pulled away. The rest of that day none of us was too cheery. The loss

of Andre had left us all a little depressed, and we could visualize Thomas sitting alone in his house that evening.

It was almost closing time and getting dark when my boss called in after finishing a horse call. He had found two tiny kittens at the intersection of two gravel roads on his way home. The fate of their mother was unknown, but they were hungry and cold. He had scooped them up and was bringing them into the clinic for the night. "I think we'll need some help with these two," my boss said as he carried in the kittens. "What do you suppose Thomas Gertsen is up to tonight?"

Agreeing that we would be too busy to care for the kittens, I looked up Thomas' number and dialed. The phone rang several times before a quiet voice came through on the other end. "Thomas, hey this is Jeff from the veterinary clinic," I said. "I'm especially sorry to bother you now, but I have a little bit of a problem and am hoping you can help me out. We have found some abandoned kittens that will require regular bottle feeding during the night, and we're just too overwhelmed to do it."

There was a long pause on the other end. Then he said, "This really isn't a good time. I'm so upset about my loss . . . but Andre would have wanted me to help them. If it's only for tonight, I'll do my part."

"I'll drop them off, then," I responded. "Thank you so much for your help."

Gathering up an armload of kitten milk replacer, I headed for his house. Thomas had a modest single-story home in a mountain subdivision. The place was a little depressing tonight. Only the living room light was on, and I saw Thomas pop up from his chair to greet us. I met him at the door with the kittens in a small cardboard box with a bath towel for padding. His eyes were red from crying, and he stared downward to hide them from me.

I shoved the box into his arms, trying to act rushed. He fought back a small smile upon looking into the container, but he couldn't cover up the little bit of happiness that crept into his eyes. "Thanks again, Thomas. Could you drop them off at the clinic in the morning?" I asked as I set the cans of milk down on the cement step. He nodded in affirmation, and I hurried off. As I left, I noticed he turned on a few more lights in the house.

The next morning Thomas did not show up with the kittens. He called in about 11:30 to say that one of the little guys had not eaten very much during the night so he would work with the kitten for the rest of the day. He would definitely bring them back the next morning, however. But the next day came and went with no sign of Thomas or the kittens. Finally, on the third day Thomas called the clinic and wanted to talk to me. "I'm afraid these kittens don't want to leave," he explained. "I've tried to bring them back, but they don't want to come. I guess I'll just have to keep them, if it's OK."

I told him that we'd talk it over, but I thought it would be OK. I hung up the phone and my boss asked me, "So, what's the deal?"

"They'll be in for vaccinations in a few weeks," I replied. "Mission accomplished."

That Special
Someone

Dating can be a little difficult for a young, single veterinarian. Rural areas tend not to have large populations of available young women. Combining the lack of potential prospects with long days and after-hours emergencies left my social life with much to be desired. Rural Colorado was a far cry from nightlife in the city with clubs and happy hours. Friends always had that "really nice girl" they wanted to set me up with, but these usually made for an interesting first and only date. Sometimes clients would have single daughters, but when they realized that I lived in a rented cabin and drove a practically antique Jeep, their enthusiasm waned. Just because I had "Dr" in front of my name didn't mean I produced the kind of income that physicians with a human clientele did. So I was about to give up when the new staff started showing up at one of the guest ranches served by the practice.

This meant a lot of young women from all over the country would be moving to the area for temporary jobs as they did every year,. The summer help spent three to four months doing everything from cleaning toilets to taking guests out on trail rides. Most years I don't get to know the staff that well, but one particular summer the entire herd of horses contracted a respiratory disease known as "Strangles," so my services were needed two to three times a week as the disease spread rapidly through the herd.

This bacterial ailment is typically carried in by a new horse and spreads like wildfire from there. This incredibly contagious affliction earns its name because it most commonly affects the lymph nodes around the lower neck, causing them to fill with pus and press against the windpipe. It is typical to see Strangles horses standing around the corral with their necks straightened out trying to get air. Fortunately, most of these animals are fairly easy to treat, but the cure is not for the weak stomached. The pus-filled lymph nodes must be drained, allowing the copious amounts of stinky white fluid to escape. Antibiotics are often used in severe cases.

Due to the frequency of my visits to the ranch that summer I got to know the staff a little better than usual, especially one of the wranglers. Marion was a beautiful blonde with big brown eyes and a great, warm smile. She had extremely short hair, which I didn't think much about at the time, but after a little reconnaissance I found out that she had survived cancer and a liver transplant during the past year. She was only 21 at the time. After this life-changing experience, Marion turned down a banking job in New York and headed for Colorado. She wanted to do something totally different to help with her recovery—fortunately for me, as it turned out.

We became friends as the summer progressed, and she decided to stay into the fall, long after the rest of the staff would have returned to college. She had already graduated, so I had time to develop a game plan without appearing overly interested. The truth is, it got to the point where I was making up reasons to show up at the ranch and see Marion. But I had to walk a fine line or someone might catch on. One advantage of being a single, over-30 male is learned patience when it comes to dating.

My opportunity eventually came when an overly aggressive suitor showed up to take her out one fall evening when I happened to be at the ranch. Marion wanted me to act as if she and I already had plans to get her out of her date, so I played it casual. "Well, I guess if it will help you out . . . I could take you out to dinner." This nonchalant attitude could have backfired, I realize now, but in this case it worked as planned. Within a few weeks we were dating, but her time at the ranch was quickly running out as the tourist season came to an end. She headed home over the holidays for a month of which I missed her every second. In January she was back in Colorado, and before we knew it we were an item.

Usually, I'd reach a point in the dating process (which I had begun to call anything that lasted past a date or two) when I would begin looking for things not to like in the current girlfriend. But this time there seemed to be nothing to dislike, and this was making me more than just a little nervous. Marion was obviously a very special person to have lived through what she had, and she had a great attitude about life. We also had very similar interests, including a mutual love of animals—an important attribute if you're going to spend a lot of time with a veterinarian.

Both of us will always remember the first time Marion was with me when I had to see a sick patient. The client had called saying she needed to bring in a newborn calf with severe diarrhea. When she pulled up the clinic driveway, we discovered the calf wasn't in a live-stock trailer as one might expect. Instead, it was in the rear of the brand-new Volvo station wagon that also held the owner and her five kids. Needless to say the interior was covered with bovine fecal material and the acidic stench that goes along with it. A trade-in was definitely in the near future for the family.

I treated the calf while it was still in the car and sent them on their way. This wasn't much of a romantic date, but Marion thought it made a good story for the folks back in Connecticut.

Over the next two years we spent as much time together as possible. While I worked she took classes to become a physician's assistant or "P.A." Inevitably, we came upon the time in the relationship to meet family and friends. We decided to start with my parents, so we took the train to Iowa.

As with any typical parent-meeting affair, the first thing we did after getting off the train was sit down for a meal. Eating seems to relax some of the pressure as long as one of you doesn't throw up during the main course. We found my parents' favorite restaurant in town, and the nervous chit-chat began. After about 15 minutes of lively conversation, Marion got up for more Jell-O salad, leaving me alone with my folks for the first time that trip. My father took the opportunity to lean across the table, stick a stern finger in my face and, in an authoritarian voice, say, "You be nice to *this* girl!" My mother agreed. Now that I knew how they felt, I could finally relax— the trip was a success!

Next it would be my turn to be under the microscope and experience her world, one that I was not at all familiar with or prepared for. I figured I was not apt to be received nearly as well as Marion had been and started creating failure scenarios in my head. Connecticut might well have been another country, for all I knew, and I decided the best I could hope for was not to be sent home early.

A couple of months later it was time to go. We would not only meet her family but also attend the wedding of an old friend of Marion's, a whole other story that I'll get to shortly. Marion's father and stepmother picked us up at the airport. greeting me with open arms and appearing not to be terribly disappointed. We spent the next two days with them and their beautiful hunting dogs, getting to know each other while doing a little sightseeing in the Northeast. Being on better than your best behavior for 48 hours can be a little exhausting, but this was one of those times in life when I just had to stay the course. The alternative would have been the silent treatment on the plane ride home and a quick breakup in the terminal back in Denver, a thought too terrible to even contemplate.

We had a great time, and in a couple of days they dropped us off at Marion's mother's house for the second round. Marion's stepfather was recovering from hip replacement surgery, and he tottered out to shake our hands. Her mother stepped out the front door, politely introduced herself, and announced that dinner was getting cold. Everything seemed to be going reasonably well for what could have been an awkward situation with both sets of parents there. But before we could part company with Marion's father and stepmother, the dogs, still in the rear of the SUV, started whining to let us know that they needed a bathroom break before their trip home. We popped open the back of the vehicle so they could relieve themselves on the front lawn, which seemed innocent enough, except that one factor had been forgotten—Marion's mother's 100-plus-pound, un-neutered German shepherd. It wasn't the fear of a dog fight that brought about concern, but rather that her dad's prize Labrador female was in season. I was sure that a litter of well-bred shepherd crosses was not exactly what they were hoping for.

The big shepherd came loping around the corner of the house with only one thing on his mind. He completely ignored all of us and headed straight for the Lab. They began to circle each other in a courting sort of way, and after just a few seconds of getting to know each other the male made his move, evoking a lot of yelling and arm waving from the human audience.

This would have been the right time for the veterinarian boyfriend to jump in and save the day, but instead I froze. Marion's father was running across the grass to separate the lustful canines while her mother scowled from the front step as dinner continued to get colder.

It just seemed like one of those sticky family situations that a boy-friend should not get involved in, veterinarian or not. I felt it would be better to fade into the hedgerow than risk involvement. Eventually, Marion's father got the dogs separated, and Marion helped him get his dogs back into the car as one of Marion's sisters appeared from the house to restrain the disappointed shepherd. We said our good-byes to Dad and Stepmom, and finally moved inside.

Due to the long delay, we sat down to dinner immediately. It was cold as ice by that time, but we dug into it as if it were right out of the oven. I remember especially the gelatinous gravy and mashed potatoes that required a knife. At first we suffered in silence, but then Marion's sister made some comment about needing a wood chipper for the roast beef, and this observation was followed quickly by snorts of held-back laughter. When Marion's mother finally cracked a smile, we all burst into full-fledged belly laughs. I thought for sure I was going to blow the corn out through my nose, which would have made a truly memorable first impression. Thank goodness I didn't. We still enjoy laughing about that meal every time we get together.

Fish Out of Water

Most of the rest of that first trip to Connecticut was devoted to attending the wedding of a good friend of Marion's. Since I had finally met both sets of parents by that time, I was able to relax enough to notice that this was the land of Martha Stewart with beautiful old colonial homes, immaculately groomed, and quaint main streets magically protected from strip malls and big box stores. Large sport utility vehicles equipped with golden retrievers and driven by beautiful women with perfect, bobbed hairdos dotted the roads. This was a long way from the small Iowa farming community where I grew up, but fortunately, Marion had equipped me with some new clothes for the trip and decked me out in the uniform of the Northeast: a blue blazer and khakis. I was glad of it because I realized immediately that my usual dog-hair-covered flannel shirts and dirty jeans were not going to cut it here.

Even after surveying the surroundings and realizing, as they say, that we weren't in Kansas anymore, I still was not prepared for the sort of wedding we attended. The bride's father was the CEO of an international corporation, and the wedding took place at just one of the homes in their collection. It was a huge white colonial with black shutters and a circular driveway. Hundreds of flowers had been strategically placed throughout the yard just for the special day, but they gave the impression that they had grown there on their own accord. A fresh slate walkway led to the backyard where the festivities were already beginning under the Big Top. The reception was to be held in a huge white tent draped with strings of tiny white lights. It was *Father of the Bride* gone wild. In each corner was a full bar, staffed with three extremely attentive and well-groomed bartenders. Other staff bustled their way from chafing dish to chafing dish, preventing the horror of horrors—less-than-overflowing trays of pink tenderloin medallions. I sympathized with the staff, feeling a little more comfortable with them than with many of the other guests.

The bulk of the temporary Taj Mahal contained round tables draped with crisp white tablecloths. Eight elaborate place settings adorned each table, with multiple forks surrounding every plate. This meant embarrassing moments for me to come, trying to guess which one was for what. Roses at the peak of bloom were stuffed so tightly in vases at the center of each table that I thought their containers might explode.

At one end of the tent stood a long table with even more extravagant flower arrangements, obviously set aside for the wedding party. At the opposite end, large black speakers were being set up for the night's entertainment. I began to feel more than a little out of place in this opulent setting. Midwestern wedding receptions were usually carried out in the basement of the church. For a small "donation," a group of women in the church would make sandwiches, Jell-O salad and punch for the guests, while the cake was often put together by a family member. Growing up in the Methodist church, I was used to the strongest ingredient in the punch being cranberry juice, and dancing was not generally encouraged. But this was a different world, and I knew I would have to adjust—quickly. A good performance would not only impress Marion but would also increase my chances

of passing the evaluation of her friends, whom I had not met before that day. This was important since all men know that they don't stand a chance until all the girls his girlfriend has ever known have given the thumbs-up. So the pressure was on. This might be my only chance, and I didn't even have the home-court advantage.

My first faux pas occurred when I attempted to get a picture of the wedding party with my disposable camera. They were lined up for the professional photographer, so I thought it would be the perfect opportunity. The photographer was a large, rotund man with a ponytail and a tuxedo that may have fit well 10 years before. He appeared to feel that a mantle of photographic talent had been laid across his shoulders by the Almighty Himself and proceeded to yell at me for invading his art form. In actuality, he planned to be the only one with pictures of the event, thus increasing his opportunity for sales afterwards. No matter the reason, I felt a fool and took my leave while Marion posed with the rest of the blonde and highlighted bridesmaids.

The unfortunate aspect of my date being in the wedding party was that she would not be able to sit with me. Her place was with the rest of the bridesmaids at the head table. Normally this would be no big deal, but I was so far out of my element that I dreaded a two-hour dinner without her. The guests began to filter into the tent and search out their place cards. Having scoped out my seat early on, I watched as my table filled up with smartly dressed urban couples. Drawing in a deep breath, I could not put off the inevitable any longer and headed for my assigned seat.

The faces around me went silent as I pulled my chair up to the table and fumbled with my napkin. I soon found out that they all knew each other and worked with the bride in New York. Why I was seated with this group of Manhattanites was a bit of a mystery, but since I knew no one except Marion, I suppose this table was as good as any. They observed me with great interest, asking the usual questions about career and where we lived. Eventually, they came to the conclusion that I was some combination of Grizzly Adams and James Herriot. They were at least clear that I was definitely not the typical Wall Street-type they were accustomed to.

Finally, after an uncomfortable lull in the conversation and a lot of staring in my direction, one man spoke up with a question I could handle. He was a middle-aged fellow with one of those comb-overs that would not have done well in a stiff breeze. "I've got a bulldog that was in the kennel last week while we were in the Hamptons," he began, "and now he has a loud cough. In fact, it's keeping us awake at night. What do you think?" The whole group awaited my answer with great anticipation. Thank goodness it was a fairly easy absentee diagnosis, and I felt myself straightening up in the chair to explain it. The pup had obviously picked up "kennel cough" during his doggie hotel stint. It's the most common disease that dogs pass back and forth in tight quarters. A couple of weeks' worth of antibiotics and the pooch should be back to normal. The man seemed to be relieved by this information and settled back to enjoy his lobster bisque.

The rest of my table mates then began to stir as they each had a few questions about their pets' illnesses and took turns asking me for veterinary advice, everything from feline bladder infections to ear mites in dogs. Some practitioners might have been offended by being pressed for free consulting, but I was elated to have the conversation turn to something I understood. The eccentricities of the stock market is a hard topic for me to grasp. Once everyone seemed happy with my responses to their inquiries, I was no longer an outsider. In fact, they completely accepted me for the rest of the evening. Our table was responsible for the loudest chatter and most laughter, giving me high boyfriend marks for the event. But I can't take full credit—the open bar may have contributed a little.

Somewhere between the filet mignon and the wedding cake, the band started up and the dancing commenced. The lead singer was good enough to bring down the house in Vegas, and he was accompanied by back-up vocalists and several instruments. The band's repertoire ranged from *Big Chill* tunes to the best of James Brown, the kinds of songs that take you back to where you heard them the first time. It's amazing how music can bring back memories that include familiar sights, sounds and smells. Observing the people dancing in the lighted tent, I was reminded how weddings can stir up the romantic in people.

Couples who had been married for decades were pulling each other close and exchanging kisses as if they were the only ones in the room. Single women started looking at their boyfriends, maybe wondering why they hadn't been asked yet, and people without escorts just tended to drink more as the evening progressed. When the band started in on their rendition of "Only Fools Fall in Love," I noticed a couple of young bachelors staring at my date, my cue to ask her to dance.

Weddings are contagious. A year later, Marion and I were walking down the aisle. Even now, after ten years of marriage, I still can't wait to get home at night to see her.

Overexposed

More often than not small dogs spend their lives thinking they are Great Danes or Saint Bernards. They act like big dogs in small-dog suits. Unfortunately, this way of thinking doesn't always pay off for them. One of these typical small dogs was a tough little Yorkshire terrier named David. He would come to see us once a year for an exam and vaccinations. David came in with his two biggest fans—his human, Miss Davis, and his protector, Goliath. A 120-pound German shepherd, Goliath's main job in life was to keep David from getting killed by other members of his own species.

Miss Davis was an attractive middle-aged woman who was just glad that we were there for her pets. She was one of those clients that we were always glad to see come through the door because she was so happy and appreciative. According to Miss Davis, she had put dog fencing around her whole yard, but David had dug out a small tunnel so that he could come and go as he pleased. Every time she tried to plug the hole, the determined little David would just find a way to open it up again. The problem was that he loved to harass the neighbor's two full-grown malamutes. He would burrow through his escape hatch and taunt the big boys next door until they couldn't take it anymore. The trick was that once he had pushed them to the limit, David would scurry back into the safety of his own yard. He would then hide behind Goliath and yip at his frustrated pursuers through the fence. David knew they didn't have any interest in coming over the fence to take on his bodyguard.

The plan worked well until one snowy mountain day in March. David was going through his usual routine of antagonizing the neighbor dogs when he turned to make a run for home and realized that the entrance to his tunnel had been covered with snow. He could not find it fast enough, and sadly, Goliath could do nothing to help his little friend. The German shepherd barked and growled, tearing at the metal fence, but he couldn't stop the attack. Little David didn't stand a chance. The noise did bring Miss Davis bolting out of the house, and she was able to rip David from the jaws of death by beating off the attackers with a shovel.

Even a small amount of blood in fresh snow gives the appearance that a mass murder has been committed, so Miss Davis was in quite a panic when she called the clinic to tell us she was on the way in. Christie and I continued to see the patients that were in the waiting room, and about 10 minutes later Miss Davis threw open the door with the bloody little fuzz ball in her arms. She ran past the rest of the patrons and into the exam room, her eyes red and puffy from crying. She placed him gently on the table, then looked to me "Please help him, please," she said softly. "You've got to save him." I felt as bad for her as I did for the little terrier.

I started to examine the victim, looking for any major damage. The poor little guy was very scared and tried to escape the examination by climbing up his owner's chest. His little paws were scraping back and forth as fast as they could while Miss Davis leaned over the table attempting to hold him down. Unfortunately, she had worn a low-cut, loose-fitting blouse without undergarments. In her haste to save David she hadn't bothered to put on something more practical.

She didn't realize that in David's panic he was actually pulling down her shirt. The next thing I knew, I was standing across from a mostly topless woman with only a bloody terrier between us.

My face was so red hot you could have fried an egg on it. I had no idea what to say or do, so I just kept working on David's wounds. I was trying hard to concentrate only on the little dog. At no point in veterinary school was this situation ever discussed. I gave David some sedative, and he relaxed just enough to get him back to the treatment room. Miss Davis casually pulled herself back together and headed for the waiting room until we could give her more information on David's status. She was too worried about her pet to be embarrassed.

We shaved the hair away from the wounds and got David cleaned up enough to conclude that he was free of life-threatening lesions. He had lost some blood, but not enough to warrant a transfusion.

After his wounds were all treated and the sedative wore off, David started to act like himself again almost immediately. In fact, he got a little cocky, growling at another dog in a treatment kennel nearby. I

decided that it would be best to keep David overnight for observation, so we placed him in a kennel away from any other dogs to decrease the possibility of a repeat performance.

Back in the waiting room Miss Davis waited for the report, but I wasn't looking forward to giving it to her even though it was good news Facing her wasn't going to be easy after her accidental exposure in the exam room. I finally walked out to meet her, quickly spewing out the details of David's condition: "He just has some minor flesh wounds. He'll be fine, just fine." I took a deep breath and waited nervously for her reaction.

Her face widened with a big smile, "Oh, thank you so much," she said. "I was afraid we were going to lose him. There was so much blood." She gave me a peck on the cheek and headed home, I guessed to put on more clothes.

David went home the next day, and Miss Davis made a joke about how she wasn't really an exhibitionist as she paid the bill. She and I have laughed about that day many times since, but there is still a little awkwardness when I see her in the checkout line at the local grocery.

Too Much Information

I discovered as I began to practice that many responsibilities of the veterinary practitioner are not discussed in school. These responsibilities fall under the "learn as you go" category, and the role of counselor/psychologist is one of the most prominent. New veterinarians would expect to need these skills for discussing such things as the loss of a pet or a tough treatment decision, yet it's the non-veterinary-related problems that people continue to surprise me with. Sometimes I wish that I had taken a couple more psychology courses before graduation and a little less chemistry. The elements on the Periodic Table don't seem quite as relevant now, but these counseling situations come up almost daily in practice. A few of them stand out in my mind.

One of my favorites involved a concerned father. I had treated all of the Stanleys' pets over the years, but one day I was at their ranch to take care of one of their horses that was suffering from an upper respiratory infection. It was a beautiful fall day in the Rockies, and I was very glad to get out of the office to enjoy it. The aspens were just starting to turn their golden yellow, and the sky was more cobalt than blue. There was no place else I would rather have been that day—that is, until Mr. Stanley said, in his deep Barry White voice, "Doc, I need to talk to you about something when we finish." My heart sank, sure he had a complaint about something the staff or I had done or said.

Mr. Stanley was a tall man in his mid-forties with a long beard and long, blond, unkempt hair. A rather intimidating figure, he looked as if he should be getting off a Viking ship to conquer new lands, and now he wanted to discuss something with me. I rifled through my head, trying to think of what it might be. None of his animals had died under our care; in fact, he always seemed happy with the treatment they received. I dragged out the horse's treatment as long as I could, but eventually I couldn't delay any longer. I put a label with instructions on a bottle of antibiotics and leaned up against the truck, prepared to defend myself. Crossing my arms and setting my jaw, I braced myself for the onslaught.

Mr. Stanley sat down on a stump, rubbing the head of his Irish wolfhound from whose stomach I had surgically removed several rocks when he was just a puppy. Mr. Stanley lit a Marlboro cigarette, crossed his legs and drew himself back before bringing up his problem. At last he said, "Doc, I'm having trouble with the boy who's dating my daughter."

Relief swelled over my body when I realized that all he wanted was advice on his daughter's love life. He had three very attractive tall, blonde daughters, and the oldest one had just turned 17 The concern in his face told me that he was very troubled about the girl's well-being and was looking to me for some serious consultation. I don't know why he had chosen me—probably just the closest available human at the time he needed to get it off his chest.

The problem was that the boyfriend was very disrespectful to Mr. Stanley, not abiding by the dating rules that he had set down. When Mr. Stanley told the young man to have his daughter home by a certain time, the boy said he could do as he pleased, then informed Mr. Stanley that he couldn't touch him and he would bring her home when he was good and ready. My first thought was that I would never have dreamed of arguing with this protective Nordic father when I was a kid. In fact, I would have referred to him as "sir" and always had his daughter home at least a half hour early. It was unfathomable that a high school kid would mouth-off to this impressive figure.

We discussed the possibility of burying the boy in the backyard but decided against it due to possible prison terms. After tossing around several different torture ideas, Mr. Stanley decided that it might be best if he called Romeo's parents first. I suggested that the effect could be greater if he knocked on their door himself, and he seemed happy with that plan. An appreciative smile broke loose under his sandy mustache hairs as he shook my hand vigorously enough to give me tennis elbow. "Thanks, Doc," he said. "I really appreciate your time. I'll go and see them this evening." "No problem—anytime," I replied, returning his smile. Meanwhile, I'm thinking, "I'm sure glad I'm not that boy's parents."

My pickup sped down the Stanleys' windy driveway through the shimmering aspen trees, and I felt satisfaction that I had been able to be there not only for the sick horse, but also for a worried father. He actually figured it out on his own but just needed someone to run things by.

Developing relationships with my clients has always been an enjoyable part of practice for me, which often puts me in a position of being a sounding board. Many medical doctors and their patients complain that the human element has been removed from medicine due to the pressures from insurance companies, HMOs and liability suits. Marion deals with this balancing act daily in her practice as a physician's assistant. She tries to do a good job, spend enough time with the patients and still be able to see all the appointments that have to be seen each day. By closing time she is exhausted, both mentally and physically. Maybe veterinary medicine isn't that tough after all.

I have watched families go through good times and bad times, and have watched their children grow up. I've spent late nights putting the family dog back together while swapping life stories with the owner. But even after all these experiences, I am still amazed by what people will tell their veterinarian. Sometimes you realize that a conversation is headed in a bad direction and try desperately to change the subject, but you can't quite pull the client back from the edge. Some people are just determined that they are going to subject you to the gory details, like it or not. Often these stories relate to the client's own medical problems that may be completely inappropriate for me to hear. The opposite happens to Marion. When her patients hear she is married to a veterinarian, they almost always run their pets' problems by her. "Well, I don't mean to be looking for free advice, but my cat." At least animal questions aren't usually embarrassing or overly personal.

On one particular occasion I was checking a mare for fertility issues. With the help of a large speculum, I was performing a thorough reproductive exam when the client chimed in with some experiences of her own. Joni May was a small-framed woman in her late thirties with fiery red hair and bright blue eyes. I had only seen her a couple of times before, once when her basset hound ate an entire giant,

solid-chocolate bunny on Easter morning She had been very easy to deal with and extremely happy that I had saved her dog from death by chocolate. Excessive caffeine from large amounts of chocolate can actually cause a dog to have a heart attack We took care of the chocolate-loving pup, and I had been on good terms with her ever since.

But on this day she seemed confused about the fact that I am a health-care provider for animals only. She started to tell me how she and her husband had a hard time having children. Delving into the extensive testing that she had been through, she rambled on with all the vivid details of the doctor visits and looked to me as if I might have some ideas that they hadn't tried yet. I wanted to put my index fingers in my ears and hum so as not to hear any more. I guess my discomfort showed because she said, "Well, you are a doctor after all, aren't you?" Then, before I could stop her, she went into her husband's fertility history, just what every man wants discussed with a relative stranger. All I could think was how embarrassed he would be to hear this conversation. Finally, she took a long breath, giving me enough time to get her stopped. I explained that I only had experience with animals and was not really qualified to give advice concerning humans. Can you imagine explaining this one to the judge in the malpractice hearing? "But, sir, it works for horses."

Fortunately, this reasoning seemed to satisfy her, and she changed the conversation to safer topics like the septic tank problems they were having. I finally was able get a uterine culture from the mare and found the source of her reproductive problems. Mrs. May, on the other hand, I sent back to her gynecologist. I wonder if she asked the doctor about her horse.

Scalpel, Please

If I were to associate the surgical part of my practice with a human medical specialty, it would have to be obstetrics in that the need for surgery, especially in large animals, rarely occurs during office hours. I can commiserate with physicians who, bleary-eyed, crawl from their warm beds to attend to the needs of women in the throes of labor. But at least they tend to do their work in the florescent glow of the hospital delivery room, coming in to don the sterile gloves in the nick of time to catch the emerging head. This, after the obstetrical nurse has called the anesthesiologist, monitored the newly placed epidural, and placed the sterile drape. In the case of a cesarean section, the patient is whisked away to the surgical suite and attended to. God willing, all goes well and mother and child are reunited, face to face, with either form of delivery.

In mixed animal practice surgical procedures are not as tidy as one might desire. I've always imagined performing surgery on a horse or cow and yelling out "clamp!" like a medical doctor on a hospital television show, then having some smiling nurse actually hand me one. Much to my disappointment, this is nothing more than a fantasy in the world of veterinary surgery. I'm usually lucky if I can find the appropriate tool at all. I've grown accustomed to holding a dirty flashlight in my teeth as I rifle my sterile surgical pack in a low-lit barn.

I have been on more calls than I care to remember when my fingers were so cold I couldn't feel them while suturing a cut horse or bringing a calf into the world through an incision in the mother's side. During these situations, the anesthesia is also the veterinarian's responsibility, so no one else can be blamed if the correct level of sedation is not achieved. Too little can result in a swift kick to the head, and too much can make for a very disappointed owner due to dangerous results for the animal. This is one of the reasons I always work very hard to avoid having to perform a cesarean section on an animal, encouraging the baby to come out the natural route if possible. On one particular January evening in the Colorado mountains, however, this just wasn't going to happen.

I was called out to a small ranch in a picturesque valley at the base of Mt. Evans. I had only been practicing in the region for about a year, but the Cunninghams were already good clients. They had several horses, a pack of dogs of assorted sizes and about 10 cows. The cattle were Mr. Cunningham's project, and he had just enough of them, in his mind, to call himself a rancher. In real life he was an engineer who traveled a lot as a consultant. He was the tall, dark, silent type, who, instead of speaking, preferred to leer over his glasses in a mistrusting way. I always felt he never fully agreed with my diagnoses, producing more leering whenever I handed him the bill. His wife was left to handle the animals and ride herd over their six children whenever Mr. Cunningham was traveling for work. Fortunately, they had a beautiful log home that would have fit well in a fancy resort town like Aspen to kennel the dogs and children.

Mrs. Cunningham's name was Lizzy, and she was a transplant from Southern California who came during the period when it appeared the whole state was migrating to Colorado. She seemed to love her life here in the Rockies and, unlike her husband, was extremely easy to deal with. She was always happy to see me and acted as if she got the best out of every day. A willing work partner in life for her husband, she didn't mind getting her hands dirty or getting the occasional horse or cow tail in the face.

She did have one interesting trait she carried with her from her California days that she just couldn't seem to shake, and that was her clothes. No matter what the weather was like or how muddy the corral, she always wore her designer wear. I looked forward to seeing what she would come out of the house in. The wardrobe usually included designer jeans, an Ann Taylor top and flip flops. In these she would head down to the barn lot to wrestle a horse or cow. She was a great help, never backing away from a beast in need yet somehow managing to keep her attire perfectly clean. My clothes would usually be covered with blood and fecal material after caring for an animal, yet she was still clean enough to have tea with the First Lady. Lizzy and I had a good working relationship, so when she paged me on this night I was a little disappointed to hear that it would be Mr. Cunningham helping me deliver the calf this time.

He met me in the field near a grove of ponderosa pines. The cow was lying down in the snow, straining with labor and not making any progress. Two larger-than-normal hooves stuck out behind her, but there was no sign of a head or snout. Mr. Cunningham nodded to me, allowing his glasses to slide down his nose. I stared into his chiseled face and then got to work.

I put on the traditional long plastic glove and slathered it in lubrication. Next came one of my least favorite things: kneeling in the snow and not knowing how long it would be before I could put on a dry pair of pants. Within seconds the melting snow penetrated my jeans and the cold crept in. Thrusting my hand into the cow, I could feel the moist nose of the calf at the far end of the birth canal. Then came that sensation that always makes my heart jump—it tried to suck on my finger. The calf was still alive, but it was a long way from entering the world.

It wasn't long before Mr. Cunningham was growing very impatient, kicking the snow about with his feet. I wanted to say, "Will someone please remove this man and send him to the father's waiting room?" I was still kneeling there in the snow as Mr. Cunningham began clearing his throat. Eventually, he spoke "Well, let's get on with it. Can't you get the calf out?" I didn't respond right away. Having your arm wedged between a calf's skull and a cow's pelvis tends to make you a little less accepting of criticism or advice than normal, I've discovered. From my vantage point beside the cow, with my jeans now stiffly frozen, I wondered what I was thinking becoming a veterinarian. I was pretty sure the business majors I went to college with were tucked into bed by now and weren't staring at Mr. Cunningham, wondering what to tell him. Oh, to have a desk, a 401K plan with a percentage supplemented by the company, and clean shoes, was what I was thinking about to keep my mind off the sting of the snow on my knees.

But I gazed up at the stars in the clear Colorado sky and the moonlight bouncing off the snow on Mt. Evans, reminding me that it wasn't such a bad place to be after all. Then Mr. Cunningham's throat clearing cut the crisp air—just what I needed to snap me back to the task before me. "The calf is too big. It's going to have to come out the side," I told him.

Mr. Cunningham appeared to be shocked. "What on earth do you mean?" he responded, wide eyed. This was the most emotion he had ever shown in my presence. He was the kind of man who tried to act like he knew a lot about livestock but truly had a sparse acquaintance with the subject. This small ranch was a hobby for him, allowing him to talk like a cattleman when the flight was long or the conversation lulled.

"We'll have to perform a cesarean section on the cow right here or we're going to lose them both." As I heard myself say these words, it sunk in how much work was ahead of me. The prospect of opening up his cow and removing a calf in the middle of a snow-covered field silenced Mr. Cunningham. I was also sure he noticed my use of the word "we," inferring that he would be helping.

"I don't know, I just don't know," he repeated. I knew I had him on the run now. The superiority had left his voice, and he sank to my level.

"Well, we don't really have any choice, do we? They'll both die without the operation" He finally shrugged his shoulders, admitting that he was no longer calling the shots—nature was.

I dragged the surgery pack out of the truck and produced an injection of tranquilizer to make the cow's life easier. The sting of

the needle stimulated her to get to her feet, so we tied her head to a tree in order to keep her around for the operation. An old stump that stuck out just above the snow would have to act as an instrument stand, and the moon along with my headlights would substitute as surgical lights. Next, I infused the local anesthetic into the cow's side and clipped away the hair. With very few species of domestic animals could you pull off this surgery in the middle of a meadow, but fortunately, cows seem to tolerate it beautifully.

One of my professors used to joke that one could spit into a cow's abdomen and it wouldn't affect the end result, but none of us ever tried it. I sterilized the surgical sight with a soapy Betadine-soaked gauze pad and was just ready to drape it off when Mr. Cunningham thrust his dirty hand right smack in the middle of the freshly scrubbed area.

"Is this the spot where we're going to cut?" he asked. Now it was my turn to leer.

"Yes it is, but let's not touch it again," I mumbled. He drew back out of the light, and I commenced with another vigorous cleansing.

Finally, I pulled on the stiff, cold surgery gloves and made the incision. Warm blood oozed onto my hands, temporarily thawing my frozen fingertips. I cut quickly through the muscle layers, exposing the uterus. By now the cow had dug through the snow and was chomping on the dead grass below. After the sedative kicked in she was totally oblivious to the fact that she was a patient.

Mr. Cunningham, who had been watching from afar, was about to become an active participant. "Please put on those extra gloves on the end of my tailgate and give me a hand," I said. I could tell he wanted to give me one of his looks, but he abstained. He donned the gloves and helped me pull the uterus through the incision just enough to get the calf out without allowing fluid back into the cow's abdomen. He held it in place while I incised the uterus and pulled out the calf. Its coat was slimy and matted, and the ears lay flat against its head. There were no signs of life.

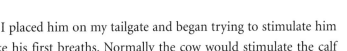

I placed him on my tailgate and began trying to stimulate him to take his first breaths. Normally the cow would stimulate the calf with a good, thorough washing with her rough tongue. Our mother remained comfortably numb, however, detached from her primal instincts thanks to the anesthesia.

After a good rubdown with a towel and a couple of handy pine needles stuck up his nose to stimulate breathing, the lifeless form at last shook his head and began to breathe. Normally, this was a celebratory event for me, but snowflakes had begun to fall. Layers of cow abdomen awaited closure, and Mr. Cunningham was getting grumpy, holding a cooling uterus in his own cooling hands. I closed the womb, pushed it back into the warm abdomen and put him to work drying off the calf. A veterinarian I had worked with as a student gave me the sage advice to "always give the tough ones a job to do to keep them out of your hair!" Mr. Cunningham got to work, rubbing the calf with dry hay.

The snow came down harder as I sutured like some kind of cruel prank. Towards the end I was blowing the snow out of the incision between every suture and digging through three inches of it to find my instruments. At last the final skin suture was placed, and the cow was struggling to get up. Thankfully, the sedation had held on until the very last minute.

To give the newborn a better chance, I squeezed some warm milk from the mother's udder into a large syringe. The sedation was completely worn off by now, and not being a dairy cow used to being milked, she immediately shot a back leg like a piston near my head.

The first milk an animal produces upon giving birth is packed with carbohydrates and proteins. This fluid, known as colostrum, is the closest thing to magic I have ever seen. Squirting it down even a very weak youngster can literally bring it back to life, and this little guy was no exception. Within a minute of feeding the calf this gift of life, he shook himself off and stood up looking for more. We untied mom, and the two ran off into the storm. I knocked the snow off all my tools and packed them away in the truck, planning to clean up the mess the next morning in the warmth of the clinic. I informed Mr. Cunningham that the sutures would need to come out in two weeks and opened the truck door to make my escape when I heard the throat clearing start up again. I thought this was it—he was actually going to thank me—but instead he grunted, "You forgot this," and handed me a blood-soaked towel Then he also vanished into the night.

I was wet, freezing and wishing the hot air would start coming out of the vents in my pickup. I think my heart was even becoming a little frozen as I sat, wondering what career I should try next, when a steaming mug in the cup holder caught my attention. It was filled with hot chocolate, and beside me on the passenger seat was a bag holding a dozen still-warm chocolate chip cookies. Mrs. Cunningham had snuck down with these treats while I was finishing up the surgery. I gulped at the cocoa and inhaled the cookies. By the time I pulled in our driveway, I found Marion had left a light on, and the cocoa had brought me back to normal body temperature. It was enough to make me think that veterinary practice wasn't so bad after all, and I could stick with it a little longer.

Collateral

Most of us who go into veterinary medicine looking forward to helping sick and injured animals don't initially think about things like getting paid or how to deal with bad accounts. Most clients are really good about paying, but every so often an uncomfortable situation arises concerning a bill A few unpaid bills here and there don't seem like they'd be that big a deal, but they add up over time. What people forget is that we have not only worked hard to save their pet or livestock, but may have used expensive medications that have to be replaced. And to top things off, the staff likes to get paid occasionally. If practicing for free becomes the rule rather than the exception, bankruptcy and foreclosure are not far behind, which means that the veterinarian will no longer be around to look after the welfare of the animals.

Most veterinarians try to prevent this problem by coming up with innovative ways to ensure they get paid. Some practitioners turn to collection agencies. While I've found these can be used as a last-ditch effort, what has worked well for me is taking collateral. If clients leave behind an item that they want back badly enough, they almost always seem to come up with the money. Being a rather non-confrontational person, I can find it hard to bring up the subject of payment, let alone collateral, but it has become a necessary evil. An interesting aspect of taking people's material belongings in hopes they will eventually want them back is seeing what they consider valuable. Over the years I have collected everything from leather jackets to diamond broaches, and fortunately I've traded nearly all of the items back for payment of clients' bills.

One summer morning Marion and I were halfway through our Wheaties and the *Today Show* when an emergency page came through from a Mrs. Gordon. "I'm a little embarrassed," she began, "but my cat Tom had a kitten about an hour ago and is straining as if more are coming. We just thought Tom was getting a little overweight. I guess we'll have to rename her." She continued to tell me that she had not been a client of ours before and that she had no money right then to pay for our services. Her husband had already gone to work, but he would be able to take care of the bill on his way home.

By this point in my career I had heard all the lines at least twice and was becoming a little skeptical of humankind. I thought for a couple of moments and decided to hedge my bets a little. "Do you think you could maybe bring in some collateral until you husband can come by?" I asked.

Now it was her turn to hesitate "Well . . . I guess I could come up with something. Yes, I know just the thing."

"Great," I replied, always hopeful. "I'll meet you at the clinic and we'll see what we can do for old Tom." I hung up the phone wondering what "valuable" item she would show up with.

It was one of those mornings that, although it sounds sappy, makes you just glad to be alive. The sky was azure blue without a single cloud to break it up, a treat that Colorado seems to supply on a fairly regular basis. It was well before office hours, so I took a seat behind the front counter of the clinic to wait for Mrs. Gordon. I was beginning to bob my head a little when her custom van roared up the driveway, sliding to a stop at the last minute. Within seconds she popped out the driver's side door with a cat carrier in her left hand, a baby in the crook of her arm, and a 30-06 high-powered hunting rifle in her right hand—an interesting choice for collateral. I hurried to hold the door open for her as a man with any sense would for a woman packing that much heat. She laid the rifle down on the exam table beside the straining cat. I quickly toted the weapon off to the back office just in case things didn't go quite as planned.

Tom's one live kitten was already enjoying a buffet of milk all to herself, but no more siblings were appearing. I examined the birth canal, hoping to find a head or a tail to get a hold of and slip out into the world, but no such luck. At this point we had two choices: a cesarean section or an injection to encourage the cat to push the kittens out the natural opening. Most veterinarians choose the conservative route first, so I reached for the bottle of oxytocin first. Ptocin, as it is known in human medicine, causes the uterus to start contracting again even when the organ has given up from hours of labor.

Eventually the injection kicked in, and Tom started to become uncomfortable from the straining. This time my examination revealed a tiny white tail and a pair of mouse-like pink rear feet. After putting on some sterile gloves I was able to get one of the feet between my index and second finger and began to tug at the reluctant little animal. Pulling on the leg with only two fingers got to be tedious quickly, yet the kitten seemed to get a little closer to coming into the world with every try, so I kept after it. Just when my fingers were starting to cramp, the kitten popped out into the world like a cork off a wine bottle.

"Is it alive?" Mrs. Gordon whispered. This was the question I always heard the second any newborn came into the world. The miracle of birth has never worn off for me, no matter what species it is, but the elation is stifled when there is a question of life. This tiny feline wasn't moving, and his tongue had a tinge of blue. I placed him on his side, cleaned the mucus out of his mouth, and pumped gently on his chest with my fingers. After several pumps, oxygenated blood returned to the tongue, and the infant cat began to wiggle. It

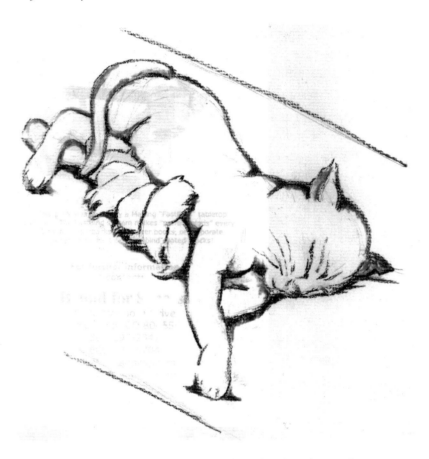

coughed a couple of times, shook its fuzzy head, and started moving towards the milk bar.

While I was resuscitating the kitten, four more fuzz balls had appeared on the table. The breech one had been holding up the show, and once he was out of the road the rest found their own way. Now Mrs. Gordon really had her hands full: seven new babies including the human one.

I helped her pack them up and get them all back in the van, just in time because someone needed a clean diaper and other clients would be coming in soon. Just before slamming the rusting van door, she called out, "My husband will be in this evening to settle up."

"I'll believe it when I see it," I mumble after the door was safely closed.

Lorraine, our receptionist, walked in as the Gordon clan pulled onto the highway. She turned up her nose and began cleaning up the exam table. "You had an early start," she said with a sneer. She always appeared to get great enjoyment out of my long hours. In reality she was more valuable to the practice than an inexperienced veterinarian like me, and she knew it. There were innumerable young veterinarians who would love to practice in Colorado, but a good, organized receptionist was hard to find.

The rest of the day was rather uneventful—a couple of elective surgeries and a lame llama in the afternoon. We were just about ready to close the doors at seven p.m., hours we kept for the convenience of those who could only make it in after their work day. Christie was trying to get away for another "big date" while Lorraine called home to see what she needed to pick up on the way.

I was beginning to wonder what the rifle in the back was worth when a pickup tore up the driveway. It was one of those souped-up varieties with oversized tires and silhouettes of provocative women on the mud flaps. It even had a gun rack in the rear window that was missing its gun. The clinic door flew open and a large man stepped in looking a little agitated. He had a mullet haircut and an orange baseball cap with a buck deer on the bill. By the look of things, he didn't like wasting money on shaving razors, maybe saving it instead for beer.

"My wife said she left my rifle here, and I'm here to get it back," he began without even saying hello.

I squelched the urge to run back to the office, grab the rifle and give it back to him without asking for any form of payment, then apologize profusely and hide behind my desk until he left. Instead, I managed to hold my ground. "Thanks for coming in, Mr. Gordon," I said, trying to sound both casual and cheerful. "We were able to save all of Tom's kittens and Tom, too."

He hesitated for a minute, then spoke again. "But we thought that Tom was . . .?" "I know, but that's an easy mistake to make. We even confuse young kittens here at the clinic occasionally."

His expression began to soften, maybe thinking of his baby daughter playing with the squirming newborn kittens at home. "I guess I would miss that old cat if anything happened to him . . or her. It's just that the rifle was my father's, who died last year, and it's the only thing I have left that was his."

Nodding sheepishly, I went to get the rifle while Mr. Gordon wrote out a check for the bill and gave it to Lorraine. I felt somewhat remorseful about taking his rifle hostage. Evidently, I should have had more faith. He thanked us profusely and headed for home with his keepsake restored. I sent Lorraine on her way. As I locked up, I thought about what a pity it is that a few people's dishonesty leads to dilemmas like this for the rest of us.

Contagious

I can't understand what this man is talking about," the receptionist said, pointing to the phone with the hold light flashing. "It's something about a cat and maybe hair loss. You try and talk to him."

When I picked it up, the voice on the other end spoke in a syrupy Southern accent that sounded almost alien. "How y'all doing, Doc?" was nearly all I could decipher. I did catch something about his cat intermixed with a series of words that were completely unrecognizable. I returned the phone to the receptionist and told her to have the fellow bring in his pet at three o'clock.

My boss was gone on vacation that week, a precious commodity in veterinary practice, and we had a relief vet who was filling in. With such a big demand for relief veterinarians in recent years, many practitioners make their living this way, working at a number of different clinics so the more permanent fixtures can take some time off. Dr. Sally was a fine small animal practitioner who was also excellent with the owners. She took her work very seriously and cared deeply for her patients, but humor was not one of her strong suits. This slightly intense attitude made it hard not to pull the occasional prank on her, and Christie snickered when I suggested that Dr. Sally should see the cat from Dixie that afternoon. Dr. Sally was originally from upper New Jersey, and we knew that trying to get a history on the feline filtered through a deep Southern accent would frustrate her to no end.

I caught her coming out of an exam room with a small dog tucked under her arm. She had just spent the last half hour convincing an owner that the precious miniature poodle would not expire if he stayed overnight for some much-needed dental work. Dr. Sally

reluctantly nodded her head when I explained the situation involving the client I wanted her to see for me. "What do you mean you couldn't understand the man? Didn't he tell you what was wrong with the cat?"

"I think they may be from out of town; he had a little bit of an accent," I responded. "Unfortunately, I have another appointment coming in about the same time." She sighed and conceded to work the cat into her schedule.

A few hours later I noticed a 30-something couple sitting patiently in the waiting room. The husband was dressed in a gray work shirt and matching pants with the insignia of a local trucking company over his left breast. He held his gray matching cap in his lap, stained with perspiration where the brim and front of the hat met. His wife, a robust woman, wore a clean paisley dress covered above the waist with the familiar blue vest issued by a well-known big box store. Between them was a white pillow slip tied in a knot at the opening. Something seemed to be in it, and occasionally it moved like a ghost in an old Scooby-Doo cartoon.

People bring cats into the vet's office in many different forms of containment. I have seen cats confined in everything from duffle bags to elaborate cat carriers, but one of my favorites has always been the basic pillow slip. Upset cats seem to mellow in this converted bedding, and it is just porous enough to allow air transfer, though I don't believe they are sanctioned by the American Veterinary Medical Association. I had a feeling that these were the people I had attempted to speak to earlier, and sure enough they headed in to see Dr. Sally with a "How y'all doing today?"

Henry and Missy McCoy seemed to respond fairly well to Dr. Sally's direct approach I could hear the conversation outside the other door in the treatment area. Dr. Sally began with the usual medical history questions. "How long has Mr. Biscuits had these missing patches of hair? Does he itch the bare spots?"

A couple of hems and haws came from the other side of the door followed by a "Could you say that again?" The McCoys hung on every word as if Sally was about to make an earth-shattering scientific discovery.

Our visiting veterinarian then reached under the exam table, slid open the drawer and produced the black light. This tool was not to light up an Elvis painting, but to cause the suspected fungus on the skin of the cat to fluoresce and amaze the audience. The glowing patches are always impressive, but Dr. Sally had not yet conveyed the reason for this strange sight to Mr. Biscuits' owners. Finally, the McCoys couldn't stand it anymore, and Henry spoke up. "Do you have any idear what it is, Doc?"

Dr. Sally snapped back, "Well, Mr. Biscuits has a bad case of ringworm." The pride of an unquestionable diagnosis oozed from under the door to where I was shamelessly eavesdropping.

Mrs. McCoy gasped, "How on earth do the worms get under the skin?" Sally then explained that ringworm did not involve any kind of a worm and was actually caused by a fungus.

As she began to shave the infected areas for easier treatment, she mentioned in passing that ringworm is also infectious to humans, so the McCoys should wash their hands well after touching their pet. The couple seemed to perk up at this new information. Mrs. McCoy tried to ask Dr. Sally a question, but the buzz of the clippers muffled her soft Southern drawl. Eventually she was able to raise her voice just enough for Sally to hear her and turn off the clippers. In an almost embarrassed tone, Mrs. McCoy forced out the question: "Could this be the same problem that Henry has? Go ahead, Henry, show the doctor the area that's been botherin' you."

I heard the rattle of a belt buckle, then a very upset Dr. Sally yelling. "No, no, you need to show that to your own medical doctor!" Her usual confidence and composure had abandoned her. Now she was just as frazzled as I usually was. It gave me a little warm feeling inside when she shoved open the door, her face pale, shaking her head with frustration as she ran past me. Henry's ringworm lesion was in an area that should not have been exposed to anyone but his wife or physician. The McCoys, however, must have figured they could kill two birds with one stone and save the cost of an extra office visit as well.

I asked Christie to help me finish treating Mr. Biscuits and sent the couple off to their family doctor. A few minutes later Dr. Sally reappeared from the office area where she had been hiding from the McCoys. Christie and I were in the process of cleaning up the exam room and sterilizing the Formica tabletop. We both were trying to hold back laughter, causing our eyes to water and an occasional snort to escape. To our disbelief Dr. Sally cracked a small smile, which meant the can was open. All three of us broke into a full-fledged roar that left us gulping for air.

The McCoys had managed to do what the rest of us could not—allow Dr. Sally to laugh at herself. From that day on her time spent with us was a lot more enjoyable for everyone, including Sally, and ringworm cases took on a whole new meaning.

Wild Kingdom

In the mountainous areas of Colorado you never know what you will run into or who you might encounter next. Most people are not native to the area but have ended up in the mountains from other states or counties, and a certain percentage of these people are running from something, occasionally even the law. My years in this beautiful but rugged region have taught me that the snowcapped peaks can draw a rather eclectic crowd.

I have been lucky enough to meet many of these interesting characters during my years of practice, and these encounters always make for an interesting day. Some days I feel more like I am watching myself in a movie or dream than actually participating in the situation. One day in particular stands out in this category of surreal experiences.

It started out as a relatively routine summer morning, and most veterinarians like routine. We get enough surprises on a daily basis. A feline dentistry and a sheltie with a steak bone caught around its lower jaw got things started for the day—nothing to increase my blood pressure, but it was still early.

Christie caught me right after lunch to let me know that someone needed to go to the Anderson ranch to see a horse with a rope burn before the end of the day. My boss overheard the conversation while spaying a cat in the surgery room, but he kept his head down over the patient, concentrating on his work. Without looking up he posed the inevitable question, "What are you doing this afternoon, Jeff?"

Since I easily interpreted this to mean, "You will be making this call," I chuckled. "Sounds like I'm going to the Anderson place," I said, but I wondered why he so obviously didn't want to go. It was a long drive, yet I sensed that there was more to it than just the trip.

I had only met Mr. Anderson once. He had come into the clinic on a busy afternoon with a fecal sample from his horse. Worried that worms were causing the horse to lose weight, he demanded we run the fecal test immediately. He was about 65 years old, sporting bushy white hair and an unkempt white beard. Multicolored suspenders held up his soiled jeans, and the tattered flannel shirt had seen far better days. To run a stool sample only a tiny amount is required, yet he had brought in the entire bowel movement of the mature equine—in a pizza box. He then proudly displayed it in front of a waiting room full of pet owners. He seemed to find great humor in the turned up noses and distressed faces of the clients seated around the shrinking space. I took it from him as quickly as possible, saving the thimbleful needed to run the test and throwing the rest away in the dumpster outside, but not quickly enough to prevent the clinic from smelling like a barn. I had survived my first encounter with Mr. Anderson, but today it was time for round two.

Christie and I got the necessary directions and headed out, a little leery of what we might find. In a time when ranches in Colorado were quickly transforming into subdivisions, it was good to know that at least this one was still in operation. Our destination lay in one of the most beautiful regions of our practice, on a stunning high mountain plateau known as "the ridge." Surrounded by stunning peaks on all sides, it is 40 miles wide by 50 miles long. The pass that gets you there tops out with a drop-jaw view of the entire area. A longtime resident of the ridge told me that when his great-grandfather had set

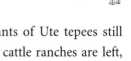

up housekeeping on the plateau, the remnants of Ute tepees still dotted the landscape. Now only the ruins of cattle ranches are left, most of which sold their water rights to Denver and its suburbs in the middle of the last century. Without water to irrigate the pastures, the remaining ranchers can keep very few cattle, and elk herds search out the sparse patches of grass.

The weather on the ridge can be harsh and unpredictable. Even in the summer the temperature can drop 30 degrees in 30 minutes in the wake of a hailstorm. In the winter the snow often comes down horizontally, thanks to raging winds, making it impossible to see even the hood of your car let alone the edge of the road. The people and animals here are tough, independent and not overly willing to accept strangers. The Andersons proved to be no exception.

The ranch included hundreds of acres, and the house sat strategically in the center of it, making for an extremely long driveway. The weathered "Keep Out" sign beside the mailbox was the first clue to what was coming. Christie turned to me and raised a skeptical eyebrow. Glancing down at the directions, she mumbled, "Hope this is the right place" I nodded with some skepticism as I headed the truck down the driveway. We drove for three long miles that seemed like 20 before spotting the main house. It was a classic ranch home, windblown with a little white paint still holding on for dear life.

Our welcoming committee was a herd of some 40 goats that gathered around the truck, bleating and looking for food. I chased them away when they started eyeing the tires. There appeared to be no humans around except for a heavyset man and a grade school-age girl lapping at ice cream cones on the front steps. They were either ignoring us or were just not aware of our presence since they made not attempt to look up from their dessert. I told Christie to try to communicate with them while I gathered together my paper towels and antiseptic soap to clean up the injured horse. It always makes a better impression to appear a little prepared.

Just as I turned to start towards the house I saw Christie coming back to the truck at a near run with terror in her eyes. She was pointing behind her as she came. I couldn't see what she was so worked up about at first. Then, by moving just a little to see around Christie, the object that had rendered her speechless came into view. Tied to an old iron gate with a thin nylon rope was a full-grown African lion. It was surrounded by a pile of sun-bleached bones, presumably from livestock that didn't make it. The scene was so unreal that I had to blink my eyes several times to make sure it wasn't a movie—something between *Of Mice and Men* and *Out of Africa*. I was halfway expecting Merrill Steep to poke her head out the door at any moment to invite me in for pie. Unfortunately, she did not, and Christie had locked herself in the truck within seconds. It was up to me to let someone know we were here and find the patient.

I yelled to the pair on the steps, "Can you tell me where I could find Mr. Anderson?" The big man pointed into the house before returning to his disappearing cone, so I gave the kitty a wide berth and headed for the front door. Inside I found a group of about 10 motley cowboys sitting around a table covered with mounds of meat and potatoes The group appeared to be a combination of every race and culture, but all were tough looking. I could have sworn I had seen a couple of them on the post office wall.

Mr. Anderson sat at the end with an authoritative posture, supervising the meal. His wife hurled bowls of food onto the table as she brought them in from the kitchen. She was a large, gray-haired woman in her early sixties who didn't seem overly happy about her position as cook, waitress and dishwasher. She occasionally scowled at the ranch hands as if warning them not to stay at the table too long. Since there was not a McDonald's within at least a three-hour drive in either direction, the patrons here appeared to obey her wishes.

I waited quietly for a few minutes, hoping someone would acknowledge my presence, and eventually Mr. Anderson raised his head just long enough to speak "Horse is in the third barn, the tallest one. Someone will be out to help you as soon as we're done here" Then his eyes refocused on a large pitcher of gravy, and I realized I had been dismissed. A nod from Mrs. Anderson confirmed it, so I headed out to pry Christie out of the truck and find the horse.

The little girl, the large man and the lion had lapsed into afternoon naps near the steps, allowing me to sneak by unnoticed. Clutching my supplies, I walked with Christie towards the tallest barn, one of many half-gone structures on the place. We ventured slowly into the building, well lit by the unintentional skylights in the old roof. Hoping not to find any more predators from the Dark Continent, we took every step cautiously, eventually catching a glimpse of the horse in a makeshift stall in the center of the barn. The animal was only about a year and a half old and obviously not well trained. He bucked and kicked in the stall, showing off for a new audience. I like to compare horses this age to teenagers, completely impossible to reason with. We decided to wait for help instead of risking bodily injury to ourselves. Christie and I sat down on a bale of hay to wait. It couldn't be long; Mrs. Anderson would surely run them out of her house soon. We waited in silence while the young bay continued dancing in the stall as if daring us to come in with him.

Suddenly, something fell from the rafters onto the floor in front of us. Startled, we both jumped to our feet and examined the object. It was some type of exotic bird, the likes of which neither of us had every seen before. The avian was rather large, about 18 inches long with a bright-red, serrated cone on top of its head and a multicolored, long pointed beak. The rest of the bird was jet black. It definitely was not a normal resident of this area. Why was it lying dead on the floor in front of us? Squinting our eyes we were able to make out the dark figures of similar creatures moving about in the rafters two stories up.

That was the end of the rope for Christie and me. We leaped into the pen with the young horse and, with the power of adrenaline driving us, grabbed the animal's halter. The horse seemed to sense that we were going to do the job no matter how much he objected, so he settled down and gave in to the treatment. I clipped the hair around the rope burn while Christie washed it up with antiseptic soap. Out of a mutual need to leave the ranch as soon as possible, we worked together like a well-oiled machine. I covered the wound with ointment and scribbled out directions on a plastic container of antibiotic powder, leaving it behind on a bale of hay by the stall.

We gathered up our tools and made a break for the truck, again giving the house the wide berth it deserved. Our escape was almost complete when we stopped short in front of the pickup. At least 15

goats were roaming about on the hood and fiberglass vet box in the back. The truck's paint was severely scratched, and the goats seemed to have done a week's worth of defecating on the windshield. At least another 25 goats, still on the ground, were trying to get onto the truck, but there wasn't any space left. Their sharp little hoofs tore at the doors and fenders. Goats are extremely athletic, even the smallest ones. On my truck they looked more like their Rocky Mountain cousins than the domestic variety they were. Normally I would have been upset, but Christie and I wanted to leave so badly we just chased the gang of caprine off and made tracks for civilization.

On returning to the clinic I sent Mr. Anderson a bill that included a little extra to help cover truck repair. Needless to say he was not happy and sent in a check that only covered the horse treatment. The envelope included a note indicating I might pick my parking spots more carefully in the future. The good news is that he never called back, and according to the neighbors, the horse recovered nicely. It's a good thing because we wouldn't have been able to afford any more auto bodywork.

End of the Day

"Colicky horse in Sawmill Gulch—who wants to see it?" It was five minutes before 5:00 p.m. on a Friday evening in mid-August, always a popular time for emergency calls to come in. This meant the lowest on the totem pole would be the chosen one for the job, and that was me. We didn't recognize the last name, but the caller was to meet me at a nearby gas station, then lead me to the horse. Why they couldn't just give me directions bothered me a little, but I brushed it off as just a new client with a hard-to-find home.

Arriving at the station I had no trouble picking out my guide. A 20-year-old, rust-scarred pickup with a large trailer hitch sat parked at the outskirts of the parking lot. One might have thought it was unoccupied except for the moth-eaten black cowboy hat barely showing above the steering wheel. Under the hat I could just make out the face of a man who had seen a lot of Colorado sun and was probably not near as old as he appeared. The hat nodded when I pulled in beside the vehicle, so I followed it back onto the road. Mufflers were obviously not a priority for the driver as the truck roared down the highway belching black smoke. Even when I lost sight of him, I could still follow the noise and smell.

I had driven this section of road many times but still had a little trouble keeping up. Just when I thought I might actually lose him despite the noise and smoke, he turned off onto a dirt road. It was Sawmill Gulch Road, and I didn't remember there being houses on it. A rough one-lane, it was really more of a path than a road. It was the only route into this region of national forest. I had been hiking in this area before and knew the parking lot for the trailhead was not much farther. The sick horse would probably be there, I reasoned, so maybe Marion and I would make it to that movie after all.

When the trailhead came into view, I spotted two horses tied to a horse trailer that had seen better days. The trailer's tires were completely bald, and paint was a distant memory. The horses had saddles and bridles on, but neither appeared to be ill. The hat jumped out of the truck in front of me and started for the steeds.

"Well," I said, "it looks like the animal is much better now. Which one was having the problems?"

The man pushed up his hat to expose the big smile that was forming across his face. "These are our mounts; the one with colic is up the trail a ways," he began. "You'll have to put all the medication and equipment in these saddlebags so we can ride in. My wife is waiting with the sick one, so we'd better get going."

My first thought was, "You've got to be kidding me," but someone had to take care of the poor animal, so I started transferring the supplies from my truck to the horse. The next thing I knew, I was actually riding a horse into the woods to treat another. I guess he just assumed since I was a veterinarian, I should know how to ride a horse. If my classmates could only see me now, I thought, they would just shake their heads in wonder. Most of them would be leaving their clinics about then to get a good start on the weekend, maybe even heading to restaurants for a nice meal. A little food sounded pretty good at that moment.

As we rode I began to get to know Mr. Ledger. He and his wife were up from Denver for weekend trail riding when their pack horse, Sue, started to go down and began to roll, the classic signs of colic in a horse. Because the equine species is not capable of vomiting, intestinal blockages tend to be incredibly painful. They can be caused by anything from constipation to an intestinal torsion, the latter being the last thing I hoped to find.

After about 15 minutes of riding, I was starting to get a little nervous. "How much farther?" I asked.

Mr. Ledger hesitated then answered cautiously, "Ah, just around the bend. Won't be much farther now." I didn't entirely believe him, but what choice did I have? Besides, it was a beautiful evening for a ride. Forty-five minutes later I began to hear noises ahead on the trail. In a small clearing was a sweaty, thrashing gray horse with a small, middle-aged woman tugging on its lead rope to get it up. The animal wouldn't budge. Its abdomen was bloated, and its pain was so great that not even an atomic bomb would have been able to distract it.

I introduced myself to Mrs. Ledger, to which she responded, "Well, I hope you can do something quickly I don't think she can last much longer, and neither can I." The two of them looked at me longingly, obviously wanting me to perform a miracle.

The horse lay on her right side at my feet, gasping for every breath. Her left eye turned up towards me with that "Please do something for me" look. Retrieving my stethoscope from the saddle bags, I proceeded to examine the patient. Her heart rate was 80 beats per minute, way too high, and she had none of the normal intestinal sounds over the abdomen. My best shot at successful treatment was to reduce the pain so the intestines could relax, and then get some laxative in her stomach.

After an injection of Banamine into the jugular vein and a little sedative to calm her down, the distress seemed to melt away quickly, and soon Sue was able to get back onto her feet. She wasn't near 100 percent yet, but things were starting to look up. During the rectal exam I was relieved not to find a torsion or intestinal twist, but there was a large amount of hard stool in Sue's cecum. This blockage was clearly the source of the problem. Being elbow deep in a horse's rectum with the requisite shoulder-length plastic glove is not very glamorous, yet it is still our best diagnostic tool for colic.

The Ledgers were elated to hear that there was no torsion. The horse would never have made it out of the forest if there had been. I got out the equine nasal gastric tube and passed it through her left nostril and into her stomach. Attaching the tube to the stomach pump, I pumped in the better part of a gallon of mineral oil, enough to loosen up almost anything! "Now we need to walk her for a bit to get the oil moving towards the blockage," I explained. The Ledgers nodded eagerly and immediately started walking the horse in circles.

After five minutes of walking, Sue started to pass gas and her bloating decreased. It was like the air being slowly let out of a balloon except that this air was a little more pungent. As the gas passed, the horse felt continuously better. A half hour later the urge to lay down subsided, and it looked as if we all would make it out of the forest that night.

The Ledgers became more talkative at this point. "Doc, you did it! She's going to make it. Thank you so much," Mrs. Ledger said as tears of joy welled in her eyes. "We never thought we'd get anyone to come way back in here to treat her." I held back the urge to ask how many other veterinarians they had called before they got a hold of me. Did they mention to the others that they'd be going on a one-hour trail ride each way?

The sun was beginning to go down over the mountain peaks as Mrs. Ledger wiggled herself up onto the now fully recovered equine. She took off down the trail bareback with Mr. Ledger and me in tow. The next hour passed rather slowly, with many obstacles that wouldn't seem like such a big deal in full daylight. Now there were low branches to avoid and hard-to-see boulders in the trail. I was certain that every bend in the trail would open onto the parking lot. It was eight o'clock by the time we reached the trailhead and a bigger-than-life moon that had replaced the day's sun long before. As much as I would rather have been home with Marion by then, I have to admit it was a beautiful night for a ride.

We tied the horses to the trailer where all three immediately commenced munching the hay that Mrs. Ledger put out for them, Sue included. I headed for the truck, and Mr. Ledger met me with his credit card out. "I just can't thank you enough," he said. "I'm sorry we kept you out so late." I wrote up the bill and copied down his information.

Sliding into the truck I waved my final good-byes, happy to be settling into the well-worn seat instead of the hard leather of the saddle. Pulling out of the parking lot I rolled down my window and rested

my arm on the ledge. I could just make out silhouettes of the horses being loaded back into the trailer for their ride home. The moon bathed the entire scene in soft light, giving it the appearance of a Western movie set.

I turned on the radio, flipping through stations until I found an old rock-and-roll station spinning a little Bob Seger. The crisp mountain air filled the cab of the pickup, diluting the smell of horse sweat that had permeated my clothes while treating Sue earlier. Back on the pavement my thoughts turned to Marion and some warmed up supper. Like so many nights past and even more to come, I couldn't wait to be home. I really hoped that the pager didn't go off that night. It would be awfully hard to face another call, but if one of my client's animals was in need, I would have to go. Fortunately, I have a wonderful, understanding wife willing to put up with odd hours and late-night emergencies. The reality is that veterinary medicine is much more than just a career; it's a lifestyle. While its demands are sometimes frustrating, the rewards of being able to help animals and their owners can't be measured.

Epilogue

The face of veterinary medicine has changed rapidly over the last 20 years. Mixed animal practitioners, those who treat multiple species, are getting hard to find. Society's expectations along with voluminous amounts of new medical information dictate that we move towards more specialization. We now have veterinarians who work on only cats or dogs or birds. Some concentrate on exotics like snakes or lizards, while others lean towards livestock. At this point I devote nearly all my time to equine practice. I enjoy working with horses and their owners but often miss the humorous situations that mixed practice can present.

Another dramatic change in veterinary practice is that women have come to dominate the profession. My graduating class was approximately 50 percent each, male and female, but today male students are getting hard to find. Just in the last couple of years women have even surpassed men in practice—quite a difference from most of the last century when veterinary medicine was considered a "man's profession."

Sometimes in the middle of the night when I am called from my bed and no one else is on the road but elk, mountain lions and an occasional state trooper, I wonder how good an idea my career choice was. Then a little girl with tears in her eyes thanks me for saving her pet or a horse that appeared near death on my arrival is munching hay when I finally crawl back behind the wheel. These are the things that make veterinary practice more than just a job. It's these little rewards that enable one to look past the impatient clients who, in the midst of their concern, feel that their pet has the most urgent problem.

Veterinarians must be able to stand up to the animal owners who want them to do something that is against their better judgment, yet be there with a hug when a beloved pet is lost. It's a profession that requires many hats along with a good sense of humor to keep from going nuts. I've learned that veterinarians need to be capable of not only laughing at the situation, but at ourselves as well.

The hours are long, the academics are tough and the pay isn't the best, but I can't think of many other professions that provide more variety on a daily basis, or more personal satisfaction. Veterinary medicine is not for everyone. I always suggest that young people who believe they are interested in the profession spend a substantial amount of time working with a veterinarian to be sure that this is the right path for them.

I hope you have enjoyed riding along with me through my early years of veterinary practice—and we have only scratched the surface.